RECENT CENTRAL BANK DIGITAL CURRENCY DEVELOPMENTS IN ASIA AND THEIR IMPLICATIONS

AUGUST 2023

ASIAN DEVELOPMENT BANK

ADB

Contents

Tables, Figures, and Box

Tables

Figures

Box

Acknowledgments

This technical paper on central bank digital currency was prepared as part of the support of the Asian Development Bank (ADB) to knowledge work on digital financial services among its developing member countries.

We would like to thank Bruno Carrasco, director general, Climate Change and Sustainable Development Department (CCSD) and Ramesh Subramaniam, director general and group chief, Sectors Group for their support and guidance in the crafting of this report. The initial draft was authored by Dr. David Lee Kuo Chuen who provided the expertise and knowledge for developing this report. He also led the refining work of the report with comments and inputs from colleagues in ADB. Lisette Cipriano, senior digital technology specialist (financial services), Finance Sector Office, Sectors Group (SG-FIN) led the effort to coordinate and contributed to the development and production of the report. Junkyu Lee, director, finance, SG-FIN provided overall directions, valuable feedback and inputs, and supervised its production. Special thanks should go to Peter Morgan, senior consulting economist and advisor to the dean at the ADB Institute, and Peter Rosenkranz, financial sector specialist, SG-FIN, who served as peer reviewers without sparing their hard effort. Their invaluable advice helped enhance the quality and the proper structure of the report. We are most grateful for their patience, feedback, and advice. We would also like to appreciate the inputs of Zheng Jincheng, Cheryl Wang Yu, Ernie Teo, Aneesha Reihana, Louisa Tay, Edward Phua Jia Hao, and Rohanshi Vaid for research assistance on this project.

The report was produced with the support of a team of ADB consultants comprising Eric Van Zant as editor, Lawrence Casiraya as proofreader, Jonathan Yamongan for typeset and layout, and Claudette Rodrigo for the graphics design of the cover. Katherine Mitzi Co, associate operations analyst, SG-FIN and Matilde Mila Cauinian, operations assistant, SG-FIN provided valuable administrative support.

ADB greatly acknowledges all these contributions.

Abbreviations

AI	artificial intelligence
ASEAN	Association of Southeast Asian Nations
BIS	Bank for International Settlements
BOT	Bank of Thailand
CBDC	central bank digital currency
DCEP	digital currency electronic payment
DLT	distributed ledger technology
e-CNY	electronic Chinese yuan
ECB	European Central Bank
G20	Group of Twenty
G7	Group of Seven
HKMA	Hong Kong Monetary Authority
IMF	International Monetary Fund
KYC	know your customer
mCBDC	multiple CBDC
MAS	Monetary Authority of Singapore
P2P	peer to peer
PBOC	People's Bank of China
RTGS	real-time gross settlement
SWIFT	Society for Worldwide Interbank Financial Telecommunication
US	United States
UTXO	unspent transaction output

Executive Summary

As different forms of digital currencies emerge as the associated technologies advance, an increasing number of central banks are researching and developing sovereign digital currencies or central bank digital currencies (CBDCs) as one way to overcome the challenges of payment efficiency, financial inclusion, and access to services in Asia and the Pacific and other regions.

CBDCs may allow central banks to tap the benefits of new digital technologies while retaining the power of a primary regulator, and might be more efficient than traditional fiat money in transfer fees, time reduction, and reach, through digitalization and distributed ledger technology. This paper surveys the latest developments in CBDCs and their features and implications, with particular regard for Asia and the Pacific.

Asia's diverse countries encompass developed regions served by good connectivity and payment infrastructure, to remote or underdeveloped areas hindered by poor digital services and weak access to financial services. And digital currency is a form of currency that exists only in digital or electronic form that may be (i) issued by and is a direct liability of the central bank; (ii) approved, authorized, or regulated, but not issued by the central bank; or (iii) operated by organizations independent of a central bank.[1]

The paper focuses on type (i) and type (ii). Type (i) digital currencies, also known as CBDCs, are central bank issued and type (ii) are central bank approved, authorized, or regulated digital currencies. The main difference is that the former is a digital form of fiat currency that is a liability in the central banking accounting system, while the latter is a form of digital money fully backed by either the local or other fiat currencies, which can be approved by central bank and/or issued by private enterprises.[2] However, computer codes or private entities could also create digital currencies backed by fiat currencies not regulated or beyond the control of the government. Type (iii) falls outside the scope of this paper.

Asian central banks have been focusing on CBDCs that address several issues:

(i)   payment versus payment to ensure finality in financial transactions involving different fiat currencies (cross-border transactions),

(ii) delivery versus payment associated with the payments and delivery of the assets in ensuring final settlement in a transfer of securities in exchange for the receipt of the stipulated payment amount,

(iii) adequacy and stability of the financial system,

---

[1]   For information, see Lee (2015).

[2]   The role of central banks operating in open economies—such as in Cambodia or Hong Kong, China—is to focus on exchange rate policy, rather than money supply and interest rates, which are endogenous. The discussion of CBDCs in Asia and the Pacific goes beyond digital currencies that are liabilities on a central bank's balance sheet. Some of these digital currencies are approved by the central bank, some are issued by private enterprises, while others are tokens on an approved payment system, such as Project Bakong in Cambodia. So far, no central bank authorized digital currency has been fully backed by fiat or is algorithmic. The latter is maintained by computer codes or algorithms with no human intervention.

(iv)   high remittance costs for retail,

(v)   financial inclusion challenges, and

(vi)   maintaining the relevance of domestic currency.[3]

The paper evaluates different CBDC options, an important subject since the design of the CBDC reflects how it is programmed to do specific tasks. The degree of interoperability determines its flexibility and enhances participation in cross-border financial and international trade. A good understanding of the design, technology, and associated risk and benefits thus helps policy makers frame the problems related to CBDCs.

However, different terminologies and the complexity of the technology are challenges and distractions. As in most technology adoption for policy implementation, a systematic process will include (i) acquiring external and internal expertise for a full assessment, (ii) initiating design thinking in a proof-of-concept stage,[4] (iii) obtaining a minimum viable product for beta testing,[5] and (iv) implementation in different stages or regions.

The report presents the definitions, models, and options for assessment as inputs into the first stage. It may be useful for those wishing to understand and explore the technical possibilities and design options for CBDCs, considering the potential opportunities and risks they may bring. Selected designs incorporating distributed ledgers with a central-bank-authorized digital currency could help reduce corporate inclusion costs with almost zero counterparty risk.[6] Whether the designs are suitable for a particular country or area depends on the needs, expertise, and available resources. The report also summarizes and explores trends in thinking in Asian central banks. The arguments from different consultation papers and reports may seem favorable to the adoption of a CBDC or a new digital payment system; however, Asia and the Pacific has still seen no official launch of any large-scale CBDC.

---

[3]   According to the Monetary Authority of Singapore, CBDCs issued by other central banks and stablecoins from large firms could be made easily accessible to businesses and households, and the attractiveness of these currencies would eventually prevail, replacing or making local currency less relevant. This is especially so in a small, open, and highly digital economy, as these new monies are designed for retail use and can cross borders, riding on the strong network effects of existing vehicle currencies and a global platform. Prudent regulation alone cannot defend against such an outcome—domestic efficiency and innovation must keep pace with global digitalization trends and standards. Therefore, retail CBDC may be a form of innovation to counter the challenge from foreign and corporate stablecoins. See MAS (2021a).

[4]   Design thinking is an iterative process to understand the user, challenge assumptions, and redefine problems to identify alternative strategies and solutions that may not be apparent with an initial level of understanding. For example, Project Ubin invited three different parties to provide a solution-based approach to solving problems of cross-border payments and settlements involving assets and CBDCs. The Monetary Authority of Singapore's way of thinking and working, as well as a collection of hands-on methods, are employed by central banks, although not all have multiple parties working on a single project. Instead, most are designing and beta testing with different phases.

[5]   A minimum viable product is the simplest core feature set of any financial technology or fintech product that allows it to be deployed. Many of the CBDC projects are split into different phases to ensure that these minimum viable products can be rolled out for testing. The People's Republic of China's Digital Currency Electronic Payment (DCEP) program has rolled out tests in different regions over different periods for its electronic Chinese yuan (e-CNY).

[6]   There are cases where distributed ledger technology reduces or eliminates counter party risks. In such circumstances, as in the case of the Project Bakong in Cambodia, there is less need for a reserve requirement, a clearing house, or a delayed settlement system. Therefore, the newly licensed corporates can be part of the payment system with no or less reserves or endowments. This lowers the barrier of entry into the payment system, with more corporates joining as a service provider to the payment system.

1 Introduction

The Bank for International Settlements (BIS) defines a central bank digital currency (CBDC) as a digital payment instrument, denominated in the national unit of account, that is a direct liability of the central bank. There is no universal definition for CBDC. The Federal Reserve Board of the United States, the International Monetary Fund, the Committee on Payments and Market Infrastructures, the Group of Twenty (G20), and the Group of Seven (G7) each have a different definition. Table 1 presents the varying definitions of CBDCs among organizations.

Table 1: Central Bank Digital Currency Definitions by International Institutions

Organization	Definition	Link
1. Federal Reserve	A CBDC is defined as a digital liability of a central bank that is widely available to the general public	https://ww.federalreserve.gov/publications/january-2022-cbdc.htm
2. BIS	A CBDC would be a digital banknote. It could be used by individuals to pay businesses, shops, or each other (a "retail CBDC"), or between financial institutions to settle trades in financial markets (a "wholesale CBDC").	https://www.bis.org/about/bisih/topics/cbdc.htm
3. IMF	IMF staff defined CBDC as "a new form of money, issued digital by the central bank and intended to serve as legal tender."	https://www.imf.org/-/media/Files/Publications/WP/2020/Fnglish/wpiea2020254-print-pdf.ashx
4. CPMI	A new form of central bank money. That is, a central bank liability, denominated in an existing unit of account, which serves both as a medium of exchange and a store of value.	https://www.imf.org/-/media/Files/Publications/WP/2020/English/wpiea2020254-print-pdf.ashx
5. G20	CBDC has been defined as central bank money in a digital format, denominated in the national unit of account, that is a direct liability of the central bank and can be used for retail payments and/or wholesale settlement. (Notice that copies the CPMI verbatim.)	https://www.bis.org/publ/othp52.pdf
6. G7	A retail CBDC would be a digital form of central bank money, denominated in the national unit of account, distinct from electronic reserves (which cannot currently be accessed by individuals) and physical cash. As a direct liability of the central bank, CBDCs would also be distinct from commercial bank money. If issued, CBDCs, as a form of central bank money, could act as both a liquid, safe settlement asset and as an anchor for the payments system.	https://assets.publishing.service.gov.uk/government/uploa ds/system/uploads/attachment data/file/1025235/G7 Publ ic Policy Principles for Retail CBDC FINAL.pdf

BIS = Bank for International Settlements, CBDC = central bank digital currency, CPMI = Committee on Payments and Market Infrastructures, G7 = Group of Seven, G20 = Group of Twenty, IMF = International Monetary Fund.
Source:
1. Board of Governors of the Federal Reserve System (2022). Money and Payments: The U.S. Dollar in the Age of Digital Transformation.
2. BIS (2023). BIS Innovation Hub Work on Central Bank Digital Currency (CBDC)
3. W. Bossu et al. 2020. Legal Aspects of Central Bank Digital Currency: Central Bank and Monetary Law Considerations. *IMF Working Paper*. https://www.imf.org/en/Publications/WP/Issues/2020/11/20/Legal-Aspects-of-Central-Bank-Digital-Currency-Central-Bank-and-Monetary-Law-Considerations-49827.
4. BIS, Committee on Payments and Market Infrastructures, Market Committee. 2018. Central Bank Digital Currencies. https://www.bis.org/cpmi/publ/d174.pdf
5. BIS. 2022. Options for Access to and Interoperability Payments, Report to the G20.
6. G7 United Kingdom. 2021. Public Policy for Retail Central Bank Digital Currencies (CBDCs).

Over time, the CBDC definition may be refined with more research and deeper knowledge from practical implementation. Different designs have also emerged, but there is no consensus for the terminology. Table 2 summarizes BIS definitions from 2020 to 2022. BIS is leading research and implementation of the CBDC within the Innovation Lab. Definitions have been evolving. However, it is now acknowledged that a CBDC is (i) a form of digital money denominated in the national unit; (ii) a direct liability of the central bank; (iii) complements bank notes and reserves as central bank money; and (iv) is accessible to the general public or provided through the wholesale network among licensed institutions, or for cross-border transactions or settlements. The latest definition refinement has also included the possibility that traditional central bank reserve or settlement accounts held by commercial banks and certain other financial institutions at the central bank as a CBDC.

Table 2: Evolution of Bank for International Settlements' Central Bank Digital Currency Definitions

Definition	Link	Timeline
1. A CBDC is "a digital form of central bank money that is different from balances in traditional reserve or settlement accounts" (CPMI-MC 2018).	https://www.bis.org/cpmi/publ/d174.pdf	Mar 2018
2. A CBDC is, by definition, a central bank-issued digital money. Different levels of accessibility demarcate two broad types of CBDC: general purpose and wholesale.	https://www.bis.org/publ/bppdf/bispap107.pdf	22 Jan 2020
3 A CBDC is a digital form of money, issued by the central bank, and in its retail version accessible for the general public.	https://www.bis.org/publ/qtrpdf/r_qt2003.pdf	28 Feb 2020
4. A CBDC is a digital payment instrument, denominated in the national unit of account that is a direct liability of the central bank.	https://www.bis.org/publ/othp33.pdf	8 Oct 2020
5. It provides a new, digital form of central bank money—a safe, neutral, and ultimate settlement medium that can extinguish all claims in a transaction.	https://www.bis.org/speeches/sp210331.pdf	Mar 2021
6. Basically, a CBDC is "a central bank liability, denominated in an existing unit of account, which serves both as a medium of exchange and a store of value." Digital form and the central bank liability are key features of CBDCs. Adopting a digital form, a CBDC differs from traditional paper currency issued by central banks. As a liability of a central bank and legal tender, a CBDC differs from private money (e.g., credit balances on accounts in commercial banks as the liabilities of commercial banks) and cryptocurrencies (e.g., bitcoins).	https://www.bis.org/events/cpmi_ptfop/proceedings/paper10.pdf	16 Aug 2021

continued on next page

Table 2 continued

Definition	Link	Timeline
7. A CBDC is a digital payment and settlement medium denominated in the national unit of account that is a direct liability of the central bank. A CBDC represents a third form of central bank money that coexists with the two other forms: banknotes and bank reserves. It is fully fungible, one-to-one at par with cash and central bank reserves. A CBDC can be categorized into three main types: retail CBDC, wholesale CBDC, and cross-border CBDC. In a simplified description, a CBDC would be equivalent to a digital banknote that could be used for two purposes: transactions and settlements by individuals and businesses in the case of a retail CBDC, and transactions and settlements between financial institutions only in the case of a wholesale CBDC.	https://www.bis.org/publ/bppdf/bispap123_u.pdf	13 Apr 2022
8. A CBDC has generally been defined as central bank money in a digital format, denominated in the national unit of account, which is a direct liability of the central bank, and can be used for retail payments and/or wholesale settlement. Based on this definition, traditional central bank reserve or settlement accounts currently held by commercial banks and certain other financial institutions at the central bank can also be seen as CBDCs.	https://www.bis.org/publ/othp52.pdf	Jul 2022

BIS = Bank for International Settlements, CBDC = central bank digital currency, CPMI - MC = Committee on Payments and Market Infrastructures - Markets Committee.

Sources: BIS. 2018. Central Bank Digital Currencies; BIS. 2020. Impending Arrival – a Sequel to the Survey on Central Bank Digital Currency; BIS. 2020. International Banking and Financial Market Developments. BIS Quarterly Review; BIS. 2020. Central Bank Digital Currencies: Foundation Principles and Core Features; C. Agustin. 2021. Central Bank Digital Currencies: Putting a Big Idea into Practice; H. Wang and S. Gao. 2021. International Dimension of CBDC: A Network Analysis; Saudi Central Bank. 2022. CBDC and its Associated Motivations and Challenges; BIS. 2022. Options for Access to and Interoperability of CBDCs for Cross-border Payments.

As different digital currencies emerge, an increasing number of central banks are researching and developing sovereign digital currencies. The European Central Bank (ECB), the United States (US) Federal Reserve, the Bank of England, Sveriges Riksbank,[7] the Bank of Canada, the Swiss National Bank, and many other developed financial centers are investigating or researching the implications of issuing a digital complement to cash or central bank reserve deposits.

In July 2021, the ECB formally launched a 2-year investigation of a digital euro. An electronic form of money issued by the Eurosystem (the ECB and national central banks) is being explored in which the digital euro would be accessible to all citizens and firms, giving users an additional payment choice with ease, and contributing to accessibility and inclusion (ECB 2021).

---

[7]   The central bank of Sweden

In the US, as in Europe, there is no decision on whether to issue a CBDC. However, the Federal Reserve has been fully engaged in CBDC research and policy development and has focused on better understanding the underlying technologies, their potential, and policy issues (Federal Reserve 2021). As countries across the globe continue their research and study, Box 1 highlights the different positions and approaches organizations have taken on CBDC.

Box: Central Bank Stances on Central Bank Digital Currencies—European Union, the People's Republic of China, and the United States

The United States Federal Reserve (the Fed) is considering the digital dollar, as cryptocurrency approaches a "critical point." It is considering the introduction of a central bank digital currency (CBDC), which refers to digital tokens issued by any central bank that reflect the currency of a country. In line with this, the Fed is investigating the potential benefits and dangers of CBDCs, focusing on whether and how a CBDC could build on an already safe, effective, dynamic, and efficient domestic payments system in serving the requirements of individuals and companies.

The creation of a CBDC would raise critical monetary policy, financial stability, consumer protection, and legal and privacy issues that would necessitate serious examination and analysis, as well as public and elected officials' engagement. The Fed plans to release a discussion paper in the near future that will look into the implications of rapidly expanding technology for digital payments, with a special focus on the idea of the Fed issuing a digital currency.

Additionally, the Bank for International Settlements, the Board of Governors of the Federal Reserve System, and six other major central banks have devised a Hippocratic Oath for CBDC design, laying out the fundamentals of CBDC issuance.

- First, CBDC issuance must be designed so it does not disintermediate commercial banks or increase the volatility of their funding sources.
- Second, this oath means that the impact on monetary policy and its transmission will be restricted as long as a CBDC is supplied in response to transactional demand for it.
- Third, while payment system design is a domestic decision, it has significant international ramifications, i.e., the threat of international currency competition.
- In keeping with central bank directives, CBDC design should focus on proactively investigating a new form of money and how it could improve retail payments in the digital space.

Over the last 5 years, the People's Republic of China (PRC) has consistently shaped its position on and conceptualization of blockchain technology, with the China Blockchain Industry White Paper of 2018, the Blockchain Technology Application in Judicial Evidence Storage White Paper of 2019, and the 14th Five-Year Plan (2021–2025) on blockchain and cryptocurrency of March 2021.

The PRC is actively promoting a more centralized and controlled version of blockchain, which differs greatly from the technology's original concept and functionality. The Chinese government is investing in both the financial and governance applications of blockchain technology (e.g., urban governance and smart city development, data management in the health and food sectors, policing, and censorship), with plans to launch a digital yuan, digital currency utilizing cryptography technology, supervised by the People's Bank of China.

The European Central Bank is also pushing forward with its work on the digital euro (i.e., a retail CBDC). CBDCs aim to combine crypto's technological prowess with the comfort of the traditional banking system's regulated, reserve-backed money circulation for regular citizens. The central bank concluded a public consultation on the digital euro, as well as a consultation with the European Parliament, and announced its intention to launch a formal investigation phase of a digital euro in mid-2021. The investigation phase will look into the use cases that a digital euro should prioritize to achieve its goals: a riskless, accessible, and efficient form of retail digital central bank money. The initiative will also

continued on next page

Box continued

throw light on any changes to the European Union legal framework that may be required, which will be considered with European co-legislators and decided upon. Finally, the investigation phase will evaluate the potential market impact of a digital euro, as well as design solutions for ensuring privacy and avoiding hazards to euro area citizens, intermediaries, and the wider economy. Within the digital euro ecosystem, it will create a business model for monitored intermediaries.

Sources: Author and Asian Development Bank; BIS. 2020a. *Central Bank Digital Currency: Foundational Principles and Core Features.* https://www.bis.org/publ/othp33.htm.

In July 2022, the G20, represented by the BIS Committee on Payments and Market Infrastructures, BIS Innovation Hub, the World Bank, and the International Monetary Fund (IMF), released a second report that examines ways digital central bank currencies can enhance cross-border payments (G20 2022). The first report, published in July 2021 (G20 2021), finds no one-size-fits-all solution for CBDCs and should be used as a guide for central banks to evaluate different options. It also suggests that global central banks should work together and consider the impact on cross-border payments during the development of a CBDC.

In April 2021, the Bank of England and His Majesty's Treasury in the United Kingdom announced the joint creation of a CBDC Taskforce to coordinate the exploration of a potential CBDC (Bank of England 2021). And in October 2020, seven central banks (of Canada, the United Kingdom, Japan, the European Union, the US, Sweden, and Switzerland), with the BIS, published a report identifying three foundational principles and four core features necessary for any publicly available CBDC to help central banks meet their public policy objectives (Riksbank 2020).

In Asia, electronic Chinese yuan (e-CNY), or digital renminbi, of the People's Republic of China (PRC), has been undergoing public testing since April 2020 as part of its Digital Currency Electronic Payment (DCEP) project. The current version of the currency requires an account with a commercial bank but may be "decoupled" from the banking system in the future, allowing tourists to access the PRC system (People's Bank of China [PBOC] 2021). On 28 October 2020, Cambodia launched the Bakong payment system built on Hyperledger Iroha closed-loop permissioned[8] distributed ledger technology (DLT) to improve financial inclusion, efficiency, and safety. Co-developed with Soramitsu, the main contributor to Hyperledger Iroha, Project Bakong is the first retail payments system globally using blockchain technology. Senior figures in the PRC[9] and Cambodia[10] have said that their new monies are not "exactly" central bank digital currency. When cash is digitized, the line between currency and payment system blurs. The fact is that individuals can now transfer money peer to peer online or offline and buy from merchants with a digital device. The G20 has established several working groups to explore potential CBDC benefits and risks. The majority of projects across the globe vary in terms of scope and timeline as several are at the research stage, with some proofs of concept, and very few are actually in the pilot stage.[11] Appendix 1 summarizes the latest roadmap of the G20, Asia, and New Zealand, respectively.

---

[8] "Permissioned" is a DLT-specific term that means users will require permission to use a DLT protocol or related system. "Permissionless" is the opposite and requires no permission to be admitted to the system as a node or participants.

[9] Xiaochuan Zhou, in his 2021 speech at the Chinese Economists 50 Forum (Zhou 2021), says: "From my personal observation, China's e-CNY is not exactly CBDC, but of course, it can also be included in the big topic of CBDC discussion."

[10] In Radio Finance (2021), Cambodia's Chea Serey, assistant governor and director general of the National Bank of Cambodia, said: "I never described this project as a central bank, digital currency. I always described in many of my interviews that it is a backbone payment system, using the DLT technology. I mean, technology wise, because it's peer to peer, and is issued by the central bank, therefore people think is central bank digital currency. It is quasi and it's not exactly what a central bank digital currency supposed to be. For instance, it is not a token based, it is account based. We don't gain any seigniorage from issuing it. We're not adding anything new to this."

[11] The lists are dynamic and readers are advised to consult the individual banks for updates.

Rather than focusing on whether the new digital currency is a CBDC or a quasi-CBDC, it is helpful to broaden the discussion to design thinking and models. This new class of modern DCEP system enables innovative wholesale and retail central banking digital infrastructure to create digital and programmable money beyond payments. For example, a more innovative design allows for settlements of payments versus delivery of digital assets and the use of smart contracts.[12]

This report also examines the opportunities and risks associated with different models of digital currency electronic payment systems given the following observations:

- Use of digital currencies and payments is increasing, driven by digitalization and e-commerce, and accelerated by the coronavirus disease (COVID-19) pandemic.
- Innovations in digital, stablecoins, and crypto payments systems pose challenges to regulators and policy makers.
- There are new payment systems that may resolve issues such as high remittance fees and entry barriers to existing payment systems.
- Financial inclusion is a key agenda for central banks in developing countries.

Making money and transactions digital, with accessibility and affordability to many citizens, effectively promotes financial inclusion. Private sector players have introduced innovative products that can better serve urban areas and the unbanked through their significant mobile and agent network expansion. Consultancy firms project the number of electronic wallet or e-wallet accounts and the fund transfer amount to increase in double digits globally and triple digits for some leading players over the next few years (Businesswire 2021a, 2021b).

As electronic or e-payments flourish, debit or credit cards and e-wallets are ultimately issued and settled by banks and are typically centralized. The banks settle payments among themselves through the automated clearing house (usually run by the banking industry) and the real-time gross settlement (run by the central bank). Previously, the central bank's focus was to keep the banks safe so that the payments would be safe (BIS 2018a). The availability of new technology, such as DLT, has prompted governments (e.g., the PRC, Cambodia, and Singapore) to search for more efficient payment and remittance services, with CBDCs becoming the focus of research and experimentation.

The structure of the report is as follows: Section 2 discusses the definitions of CBDCs and models, especially in Asia. Section 3 presents the opportunities and risks of CBDCs along with impacts on the economy and the financial system. Various CBDC models and their applications are explained in Section 4. Section 5 lays out the objectives, considerations for CBDCs, and a framework. The last section concludes with Asia as the reference point.

The Digital Currency and Electronic Payment Landscape in Asia

There are generally two types of wholesale payment systems to minimize liquidity risks and credit risks:

(i) A real-time gross settlement (RTGS) system is used for settling funds between accounts on a gross basis in real time.

---

[12] Both Hong Kong, China and Thailand have also issued their consultation papers with discussions of distributed ledger technology. See HKMA (2021a) and Bank of Thailand (2021).

(ii)   A deferred net settlement system is used for settling funds between accounts at designated times of the day on a net basis.

The offsetting of obligations between or among participants in the netting arrangement is an important issue. Another critical point is how the final settlement of funds and securities transfer instructions occurs on a net basis in real time, or at one or more discrete, pre-specified times during the processing period. Participating institutions can reduce operating costs by reducing the timing, the number, and value of payments or deliveries needed to settle a set of transactions.

On the other hand, low value or retail payment systems can exist in two forms—closed loop and open loop (Lai 2016):

(i)   A closed-loop system is a "three-party" payment system that requires both payer and payee to be on the same platform. Settlement is centralized via internal book-transfer with transactions managed by one entity.

(ii)   An open-loop system is a "four-party" payment system that transfers funds between a payer and payee belonging to different banks. There are two parties on each side of the transaction, which is more complicated when a network of banks is involved. A trusted centralized third party (also known as trusted third party) such as a card scheme/payment system or an automated clearing house batch payment system, usually appointed by the banks and regulated by the financial authorities, is responsible for processing and coordinating the transactions.

Payment versus payment is a settlement mechanism that ensures that the final transfer of a payment in one currency occurs if and only if the final transfer of a payment in another currency or other currencies occurs. Delivery versus payment is a securities settlement mechanism that links a securities transfer and a funds transfer so as to ensure that delivery occurs if and only if the corresponding payment occurs (BIS 2016). Both payment versus payment and delivery versus payment are settlement mechanisms that have cost implications. Some new payment systems related to CBDC lower the system's entry barrier, with less need to put aside liquid capital for settlement, thus lowering costs. Therefore, a good design harnessing both CBDC and the payment system's best and appropriate features may reduce friction and enhance economic efficiency, especially in regard to corporate inclusion.

While financial technology or fintech has always initiated incremental changes, new digital currency technology may enable central banks to remain competitive to deal with the digital economy's needs. In turn, successful implementation requires a good and holistic understanding of the technology, technology risks, its users and customers, and what can realistically be achieved and used. Traditional digital banking and payment technologies have built a relatively efficient financial system that serves a particular segment of society. The higher-value accounts associated with electronic payment systems are dependent on bank deposits, credit cards, or stored-value facilities, and business propositions are well defined. Unfortunately, payment intermediaries incur higher costs due to electronic payments' complexity, making it inefficient and expensive to serve a larger segment with low-value accounts. These developments serve more-developed countries well, but many potential users in developing economies are underserved and excluded from the financial system.

Not surprisingly, to address domestic payments' efficiency, new payment-versus-payment models were proposed as early as 2016 by Project Ubin to address the domestic interbank payments using blockchain technology to tokenize the Singapore dollars.[13] The project was extended to international payment in a later phase. Project Ubin, done under the Monetary Authority of Singapore (MAS), started as a public-private partnership to experiment with domestic and cross-border payment with settlement systems using DLT. In the five phases, under the leadership of MAS, several other central banks and private entities have successfully digitized or tokenized currencies, developed cross-border multi-currency models, and conducted settlement of trades with digital assets by connecting different blockchain networks with interoperable capabilities.

However, Singapore is not the only Asian economy that pioneered such an approach to CBDC. The first phase of Project Inthanon-LionRock (Bank of Thailand 2020), completed in 2019 under the BOT and Hong Kong Monetary Authority (HKMA) is a similar project with the same objectives. The second phase, or the Multiple Central Bank Digital Currency Bridge Project (HKMA 2021b), is supported by the BIS Innovation Hub Centre in Hong Kong, China and brings together the HKMA, the BOT, the Central Bank of the United Arab Emirates, and the Digital Currency Institute of the PBOC. It is a co-creation project that explores the capabilities of DLT and studies the application of CBDC in enhancing financial infrastructure to support multi-currency cross-border payments.

Recently, central banks have started initiatives for retail CBDC.[14] Real-time retail payment systems are not new, but the banking industry does not find them a compelling business proposition as it is a highly competitive business (Society for Worldwide Interbank Financial Telecommunication [SWIFT] 2015). However, central banks have been actively promoting the linkage of retail real-time payment systems.[15] From the consumers' perspective, there is a need and demand for easier access to e-money, proximity of peer-to-peer (P2P) payment, instant confirmation and notifications, cheaper alternatives to credit and debit cards, and availability of funds and access to payment information. In developing Asian economies, a mature payment infrastructure may not exist yet. Leapfrogging may occur in markets where the payment structure is underdeveloped. Regulatory initiatives formed 73% of the factors driving real-time retail payment system adoption, according to SWIFT (SWIFT 2015). The take-up rate in emerging markets is not high, due mainly to cost. Adoption is not driven entirely by market forces and usually requires a regulatory push. Digitizing cash, combined with a new DLT payment system, potentially offers a feasible alternative for developing economies[16] to unlocking the economic potential from the rise of digitalization.[17]

For an overview of the payment and settlement landscape, Table 3 categorizes the first payment and/or settlement systems of the Association of Southeast Asian Nations (ASEAN), the PRC, Japan, and the Republic of Korea. The earliest system was started as early as 1995 in Thailand. Almost all central banks have introduced an RTGS system (see Appendix 2) by now. Notably, for most developing economies in Asia, the deployment of RTGS started after 2000, with momentum picking up after 2010. Also notable is that many are researching and planning for DLT payment systems, with Cambodia the first to launch, with its Project Bakong for corporate-to-corporate real-time transactions on the blockchain.

---

[13]   A token is a digital representation of a currency or asset on a blockchain or distributed ledger. Digitalization refers to a more general class of digital representation and tokenization to representation of these currencies and assets using DLT.

[14]   As of July 2022, four central banks have launched a retail CBDC: the Central Bank of The Bahamas (Sand Dollar), the Eastern Caribbean Central Bank (DCash), the Central Bank of Nigeria (e-Naira), and the Bank of Jamaica (JamDex). According to PwC's Index, the Republic of Korea, Sweden, Thailand, Ukraine, and Uruguay have also initiated retail CBDC projects. Türkiye is outside the top 10 and Cambodia's Project Bakong is more a payment system than a retail CBDC. See PwC (2021).

[15]   MAS and the Bank of Thailand linked Singapore's PayNow and Thailand's PromptPay real-time retail payment systems in 2021, the first of its kind globally that links both countries' payment system operators, bankers' associations, and participating banks (MAS 2021b).

[16]   For information, see *Forkast* (2021).

[17]   It is therefore not surprising that MAS initiated a partnership with the World Bank and others to launch a global challenge for retail CBDC solutions (see MAS 2021c).

Table 3: Payment and Settlement Systems in Asia

Country	Earliest System Implementation	Year Established	Operator
Brunei Darussalam	Real-Time Gross Settlement (RTGS) System	2014	Authoriti Monetari Brunei Darussalam The Brunei Association of Banks
Cambodia	National Clearing System	2012	National Bank of Cambodia
Indonesia	Bank Indonesia – RTGS – Gen I/Gen II	2000/2015	Bank Indonesia
Lao People's Democratic Republic (Lao PDR)	Gross Settlement System (RTS/X)/ RTGS	2011/2019	Bank of the Lao PDR
Malaysia	RTGS System - RENTAS system	1999	Bank Negara Malaysia. The Malaysian Electronic Payment System (MEPS) is an interbank network service provider in Malaysia set up in 1997. In August 2017, MEPS merged with Malaysian Electronic Clearing Corporation Sdn Bhd (MyClear) to form Payments Network Malaysia Sdn Bhd (PayNet). HOUSe, which operation in 2006, is owned by four locally incorporated foreign banks.
Philippines	RTGS System - PhilPaSS	2002	Bangko Sentral ng Pilipinas
Singapore	New Monetary Authority of Singapore Electronic Payment System (MEPS+)	1998	Monetary Authority of Singapore
Thailand	BAHTNET System	1995	Bank of Thailand
Viet Nam	Electronic/Paper Clearance and Interbank Electronic Payment Systems	2007	State Bank of Vietnam
China, People's Rep. of	China National Advanced Payment Systems – High-Value = Payment System	2005	People's Bank of China
Japan	Bank of Japan-NET Funds Transfer System	1988	Bank of Japan
Korea, Rep. of	Bank of Korea-Wire+	2009	Bank of Korea

Please see Annex 2 for more details.
Source: Author.

Recent Thoughts, Adoption, and Emerging Trends

It remains debatable whether CBDCs could present an opportunity to initiate a holistic and fundamental shift to address long-existing financial industry issues. The following are some recent developments in Asia:[18]

(i)   **The importance of cash-like features:** Two of the most attractive features of new digital currency is the traceable offline transaction and managed anonymity. The functions will allow central banks to create a currency that resembles cash payments and yet is traceable for specific purposes. The e-CNY,

---

[18]   These trends and thoughts were first adopted in Asia in their design thinking and are beginning to influence design thinking. In particular, the adoption of some technology originated from DLT is gaining acceptance, such as hard wallet and the use of blockchain, as well as being more agnostic to the definitions and use of a system combining centralized and decentralized ledgers.

or the PRC's CBDC, has cash-like features such as offline transactions and e-wallet that offer managed anonymity. The e-CNY is designed to mimic cash that allows for the exchange of money with no connectivity to the internet or telecommunication services. At the same time, a certain degree of anonymity is retained, as in cash. New privacy technology can be incorporated in most private wallets using cryptography techniques. Some of these technologies are discussed in the second phase of Project Ubin for wholesale CBDC.

(ii) **Emergence of fiat stablecoin:** Stable crypto token or stable token is a form of digital asset backed by a underlying fiat or cryptocurrency created by computer codes known as smart contracts on a distributed ledger or blockchain. To be precise, a stablecoin is a form of digital asset or currency backed by another fiat, fiat assets, or cryptocurrency,[19] fully or partially, and is native to the distributed ledger. However, the distinction between coin and token is not usually acknowledged and stable tokens are also classified as stablecoins. The new form of digital currency of Cambodia is in principle similar to the linked exchange rate system of Hong Kong, China adopted in 1983, with 100% backing by the US dollar for the Hong Kong dollar. Fully backed fiat stable digital currency created by Cambodia may not be a CBDC under the BIS definition, but it has created an impact.

(iii) **Responding to the challenge of corporate stablecoin:** The emergence of stablecoin signals a new form of full reserve-backed currency. Facebook has proposed a stablecoin called "Diem" that resembles the Hong Kong, China currency issued under the Currency Board System, except that they are not government-backed but issued by corporates or trusts. As in the Hong Kong dollar, the existence of government-authorized notes issued by private entities is not new. As a form of money, while the idea of Diem may be practically implemented, some central banks believe that an entire class of fiat stablecoins may pose a potential threat to monetary sovereignty (PYMNTS 2020). Therefore, it also potentially threatens the stability of the global payment system, especially SWIFT in its current form. The PRC started its research on CBDC much earlier, in 2015. The publication of Libra's white paper in June 2019 accelerated research on CBDCs by central banks and especially the PRC. This urgency is due to Facebook,[20] which initiated the Libra Association, with more than 2.8 billion monthly active users as of the fourth quarter of 2020. Since then, many other central banks have followed suit. According to the BIS, about 80% of central banks are doing some work on CBDC. If stablecoins issued by licensed financial institutions overcome regulatory hurdles and are launched successfully, their mass adoption may threaten many countries' monetary sovereignty, especially smaller countries, including Singapore.

(iv) **The emergence of open and crowd-sourced design thinking:** The design of a CBDC affects the underlying payment infrastructure for domestic and international remittances. Every design has its trade-offs and significant implications. For example, emerging economies may focus on designs that will lower remittance charges, enhance domestic payment efficiency, enable financial inclusion, and promote innovation, while maintaining stability with a secured financial architecture. While individual countries initially undertook "proof-of-concept" projects with the private sector, the trend is moving toward multiple-CBDCs and retail CBDCs involving several central banks and the private sector. Some of these projects produce open-source codes and share the research findings with the public in phases.[21] The trend toward open source and information sharing may help other countries experiment with new CBDCs.

---

[19] Some are algorithmic, although a few have not worked very well recently. Notable examples are DIA of MakerDao and LUNA of Terra. The latter has lost most of its value. LUNA is the native token of Terra, a blockchain developed by the Republic of Korea firm Terraform Labs. TerraUSD, or UST, is what is known as an algorithmic stablecoin. It relied on computer codes and an associated token, LUNA, to maintain a $1 value. As the LUNA price fell, more LUNA was needed to maintain the US dollar value. No amount of the coin could maintain the US dollar peg if the price of LUNA fell rapidly. Investors fled the stablecoin, sending UST tumbling—and taking LUNA down with it, erasing about $45 billion.

[20] Now renamed Meta.

[21] For example, source codes of Project Ubin are deposited on the GitHub website: https://github.com/project-ubin?tab=overview&from=2017-12-01&to=2017-12-31; and the source codes for Hyperledger Iroha, the technology for Project Bakong, are deposited on https://github.com/hyperledger/iroha.

(v)   **Exploration of convergence of technology:** With traceability, the payment system brings transparency, empowerment, and managed anonymity by design. Combining this with artificial intelligence (AI), big data, and other emerging technologies, the advantages are numerous. According to the PBOC, the data center can provide information that the authority needs for central planning. These advantages include anti-money laundering, counter-terrorist financing, prevention of counterfeiting, lower cost of issuance and disposal, access to cheap capital, lower remittance charges, managed privacy protection, creation of new business models, and new tools for a more precise measure of economic activities and convenience. The PBOC has a CBDC design that allows AI to analyze patterns of expenditure for better information collection.

Developments and trends generally apply to digitalization,[22] not necessarily only to CBDCs. A well-designed CBDC that addresses the fear of privacy invasion using cryptography techniques,[23] may enable central banks to accomplish their mission better and accelerate the adoption of other technologies in their ecosystem. However, there may be costs and alternatives such as cash and e-money. A design that is not user-friendly and secure may exclude some and facilitate sophisticated cybercrimes. A badly designed CBDC may not be cost-efficient or could even jeopardize the financial system. Therefore, understanding which technology and design can help solve the issues, lower the risk, and alleviate the pain points is essential for finding the appropriate CBDC design. Since the problems may not be precisely the same for each country, a design useful for others may not necessarily be appropriate.

(vi)   **Focus on data privacy protection:** Governments worldwide, especially in Asia, pay attention to the privacy protection of their citizens and international data protection law. The PRC is working on its regulation and CBDC multi tier wallet designs that require different anonymity standards. Project Ubin Phase 2 experimented with different privacy protection designs with Ethereum, Corda, and Quorum DLT.

A good combination of digital currency and electronic payment may bring about a safe, efficient, trustable, cost-effective, secure, and privacy-protected CBDC.

---

[22]   For example, the metaverse economy or a virtual economy generated by and utilizing AI, blockchain, cryptocurrency, and data analytics to mimic real-life experiences may pose the same challenges to central bankers and regulators (Newton 2021).

[23]   Besides those privacy protection techniques outlined in Project Ubin, technology such as secure multiparty computation, secret sharing, ring signature, zero-knowledge proof, trusted executable environment, and others can address the privacy invasion issues. However, these techniques are still in their early stages of development.

2 Central Bank Digital Currency Definitions and Models

Definitions

The literature has extensively discussed the primary functions and forms of money.[24] A CBDC's operational system can be

(i)   direct,
(ii) indirect,
(iii) hybrid, and
(iv) intermediated.

These are discussed in Auer and Böhme (2020a). However, no precise definitions exist for CBDCs, our focus here, although multiple definitions are emerging. Digital currency is a form of currency that exists only in digital or electronic form that may be (i) issued by and a direct liability of the central bank; (ii) approved, authorized, or regulated, but not issued by the central bank; or (iii) operated by organizations independent of a central bank or computer codes. Figure 1 categorizes three digital currency types: central-bank-issued digital currency (CBDC), central-bank-authorized digital currency—both government-backed and discussed below—and others.

(i)   Central bank issued

The IMF has defined CBDC as a digital representation of a sovereign currency issued by and as a liability of a jurisdiction's central bank or the monetary authority (IMF 2020a). This definition excludes digital currencies known as synthetic CBDCs that are not a direct claim on the central bank. A synthetic CBDC is a digital form of (e-)money that is fully backed by central bank money. It also excludes any liability issued by a central bank that is not in its sovereign currency (i.e., where it does not have monetary authority). The trust of central-bank-issued digital currency must lie with the central bank directly and solely.

However, as part of M0, a measure of money supply, a CBDC would share many properties with cash besides qualifying it as legal tender.[25] The digital currency would also remain the central bank's liability, as commercial banks deposit the notes and coins in exchange.

---

[24]   Appendix 4 discusses the functions and types of money.
[25]   Different jurisdictions may have different definitions and ways of calculating monetary aggregates. For discussion here, M0 refers to the physical form of money or cash (notes and coins); MB, or monetary base, refers to the base money supply from which banks can extend the money supply. MB consists of the total currency circulating in public, plus the physically held currency in commercial banks' vaults, plus the commercial banks' reserves held in the central bank. Cash (notes and coins) are physical representations of central banks' liability. Central bank reserve deposits are book entries (or book money) and electronic representations of a central bank's liabilities to the commercial banks.

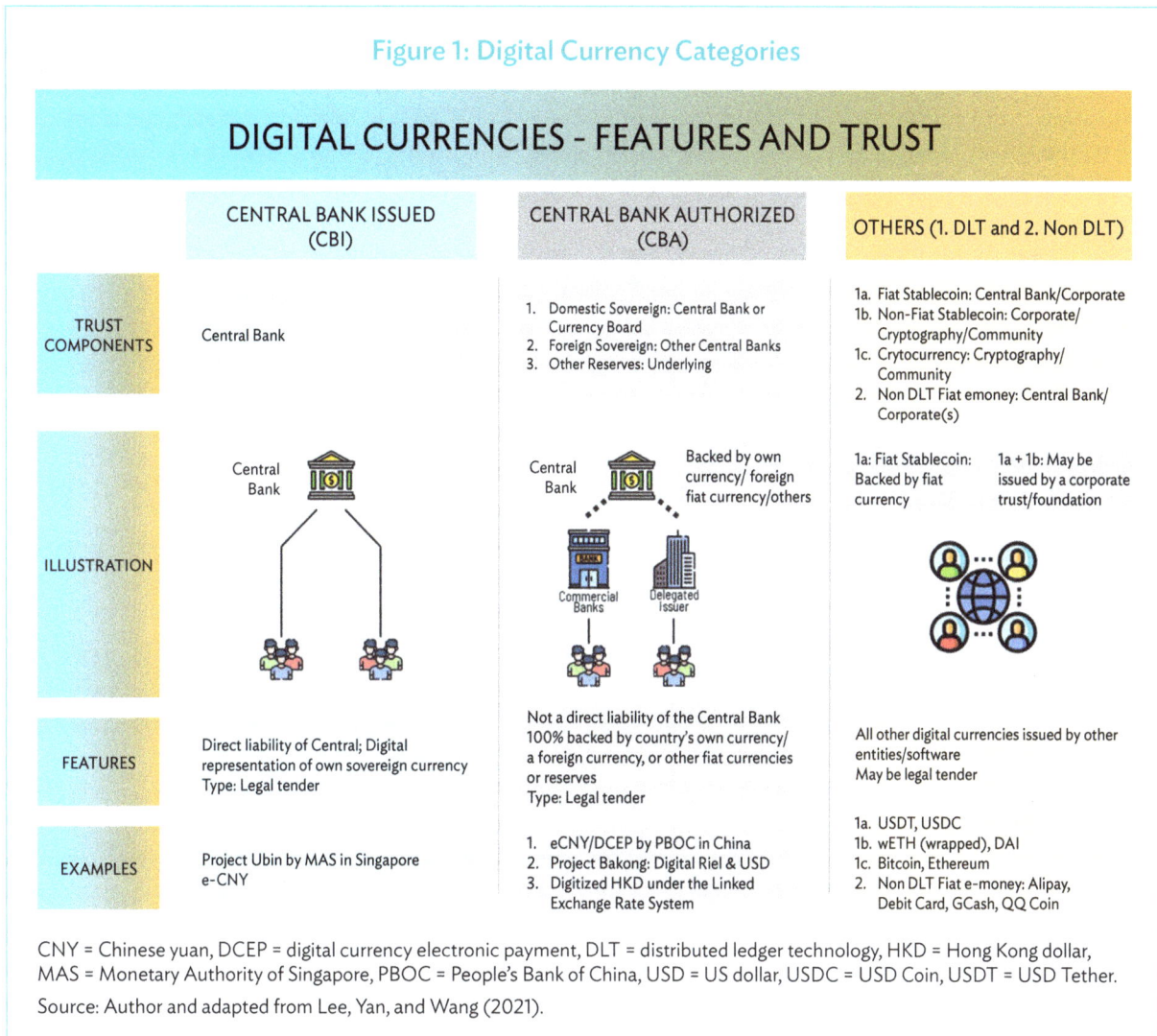

Figure 1: Digital Currency Categories

CNY = Chinese yuan, DCEP = digital currency electronic payment, DLT = distributed ledger technology, HKD = Hong Kong dollar, MAS = Monetary Authority of Singapore, PBOC = People's Bank of China, USD = US dollar, USDC = USD Coin, USDT = USD Tether.
Source: Author and adapted from Lee, Yan, and Wang (2021).

According to the BIS, a CBDC is a digital payment instrument, denominated in the national unit of account, that is a direct liability of the central bank (BIS 2020a). It is often assumed that a CBDC would be designed to have cash-like properties, including zero remuneration. But a CBDC can also be designed with attributes similar to deposits, and can be interest bearing. While a cash-like CBDC may lead to lower demand for cash, a CBDC that closely competes with deposits depresses bank credit. CBDC remuneration is an important issue for three reasons: (i) the positive interest differentiate from bank deposits may promote disintermediation of banks and affect credit, (ii) a dynamic remuneration scheme for CBDC may potentially be a new monetary policy tool, and (iii) a fully flexible remuneration dynamic system that allows for negative interest rates may affect the behavior of depositors and financial institutions.

As for a synthetic CBDC, some observers debate whether it is indeed a form of CBDC. However, Adrian and Mancini-Griffoli (2019a, 2019b) argue that it *is*, in that it is a form of public-private partnership, in which e-money providers get access to central bank money as central bank reserves, and are thus able to hold and transact in the latter. Thus, synthetic CBDC falls into our type (ii) in which the digital currency may be authorized, approved, or regulated by the central bank, but it is not a liability on the central bank's balance sheet.

(ii)   Central bank authorized

A central-bank-approved institution can be authorized to issue digital currency. One example is a digital representation of a currency with 100% central bank reserve backing. If backed by a local currency, the ultimate liability (though not direct or sole liability) of the newly created money is still with the central bank. However, if the digital currency's backing is by a foreign currency or a reserve without the central bank's control, it is not the central bank's liability. The liability may rest with a physical or digital vault or the currency board as a third-party trust. One main difference is that the underlying reserve constrains the central-bank-authorized amount, while a central-bank-issued currency has flexibility in money creation. Here are some examples:

(i)   stablecoins pegged to and backed by one single fiat currency (i.e., single currency stablecoins);
(ii)   stablecoins pegged to and backed by a basket of fiat currencies (i.e., multicurrency stablecoins);
(iii) stablecoins pegged to and backed by commodities, such as gold;
(iv)   stablecoins pegged to fiat currency, but backed by and/or tied to other cryptocurrencies;
(v)   stablecoins pegged to fiat currency, but not backed by anything, and of which the value is adjusted by automatic or autonomous adjustments of its price or supply via computer codes; and
(vi)   stablecoins pegged to cryptocurrency and the value adjusted by automatic adjustments of its price and supply.

Central-bank-authorized digital currency is usually linked to public digital infrastructure to facilitate real-time payment and settlement, separating the function of deposits and credit from payments. The ultimate trust lies with the central bank and beyond, for example, relying on other third-party trusts such as authorized corporates, vaults, and/or other monetary authorities.

In the purest form of central-bank-authorized and central-bank-issued digital currency, the fiat is issued by the central bank, of which synthetic CBDC is an example. In a more flexible form of central-bank-authorized digital currency, the fiat may be a foreign currency and the central bank can authorize other third parties or itself to allow the digital currency to be backed by any selected fiat currency. In the case of Project Bakong, for example, both Cambodian riel and US dollars are used for the two central-bank-authorized digital currencies.

Zhou (2020) discusses the differences between government-authorized and government-issued currencies. He also draws a parallel of government-authorized digital currency with e-money. According to BIS (2000), electronic money products are stored value or prepaid products in which a record of the funds or value available to the consumer is stored on the consumer's electronic device. This definition includes both prepaid cards and cash cards but excludes products that allow consumers to use electronic means of communication to access otherwise conventional payment services such as online banking. But government-authorized digital currency is more than e-money, as it also allows the latter function.

Central-bank-authorized digital currency is more a form of e-money rather than mobile banking. However, some e-monies have multiple corporate risk exposures and not all central-bank-authorized money is subject to corporate risk. For example, fintech companies may have an omnibus or general account that may or may not be segregated from their corporate account at commercial banks. In any case, users are simultaneously subject to the default risk of both a commercial bank and the fintech company.

Monetary base is a liability in the central bank's balance sheet and it is unclear whether the underlying fiat will be taken out of circulation and whether a new classification for this type of approved digital currency is needed or simply considered e-money. The first simply digitizes the notes, coins, and reserve deposits, and the latter has much broader implications. As per many central banks, a CBDC can become a third form of base money, after the central bank and banknotes' overnight bank deposits (Bank of England 2018).

While this seems to be a commonly agreed definition of CBDC as central bank issued, the IMF also rightly argues that the digital currency's taxonomy is still evolving. This lack of uniform definition reflects the different financial development stages, the central banks' challenging missions, and their changing needs. Bossu et al. (2020) conclude that the design features of the CBDC would dictate the legal framework and, therefore, their definitions. With so many variations in design, there may eventually be more refined classifications in the future.

Wholesale versus Retail Central Bank Digital Currencies

CBDCs are further classified into "wholesale" and "retail" (Figure 2). A wholesale CBDC could be used for monetary policy operations, interbank market transactions, or to purchase and/or sell financial assets,[26] and would complement the RTGS.[27] If well designed and implemented, a wholesale CBDC has the potential to increase economic efficiency within an economy and in cross-border transactions. In fact, improving economic efficiency through cross-border payments has become the main factor for motivation in CBDC research for most countries, according to a survey by BIS in 2021 (Kosse and Matte 2022). Project Dunbar, exploring the use of CBDCs for international settlements, is a good example. It was conducted by the central banks of Australia, Malaysia, Singapore, and South Africa, together with the BIS Innovation Hub.[28] Another similar multiple or multi-CBDC (mCBDC) project is mBridge, involving four economies (Hong Kong, China; the PRC; Thailand; and the United Arab Emirates) and BIS.

Retail CBDC refers to a widely circulated currency available via an e-wallet to individuals and firms for making retail payments, transferring money, receiving government fiscal incentives, and subsidies. Whether it is a retail CBDC issued via a direct claim to the retail users through platform approaches, or via an indirect claim through a two-tier model,[29] the counterparty risk and know-your-customer (KYC) responsibility lie with the regulated intermediary.

Synthetic CBDCs, for example (Adrian and Mancini-Griffoli 2019a, 2019b), have an indirect claim on a central bank (general purpose CBDC),[30] as the intermediatory bank has to fully back liabilities to a client with claims on the central bank. However, the BIS does not consider central-bank-authorized or synthetic CBDCs as CBDCs, because they lack neutrality and liquidity properties. Neutrality means that the creation of a central-bank-authorized digital currency and payment system depend on a third party. Liquidity is used in the sense that the supply of CBDC is changed at the discretion of the central bank. The intended increase

---

[26] If a CBDC has remuneration and without additional restrictions, it can also perform the function of lending and borrowing among counterparties and the central bank.

[27] As discussed in the introduction, RTGS systems are specialist fund transfer systems in which the transfer of money or securities takes place from one bank to any other bank on a "real-time" and on a "gross" basis. The alternative is known as deferred net settlement, since the netting and settlement take place after a specified period. In developed countries, wholesale payments are settled in RTGS systems. See BIS (2020b) and Lai (2018). Both the design for DCEP and Project Bakongs allows the possibility of P2P settlement as well as lowering the barrier for third-party payment companies or money transfer agencies. Both projects can be deployed as a substitute or complementary to the RTGS depending on the needs of the central banks.

[28] See Project Dunbar: International Settlements Using Multi-CBDCs, for more information. https://www.bis.org/about/bisih/topics/cbdc/dunbar.htm.

[29] In a two-tier CBDC model, the first layer is the central bank digital infrastructure, connected to the second layer. In the second tier, the digital currencies backed by fiat are usually issued by the central bank itself or central-bank-approved institutions or intermediaries. These approved intermediaries include commercial banks, telecom operators, and third-party online payment platforms.

[30] General-purpose CBDCs can be used by the public for day-to-day payments, while wholesale CBDCs are restricted to wholesale, financial market, and other intermediaries.

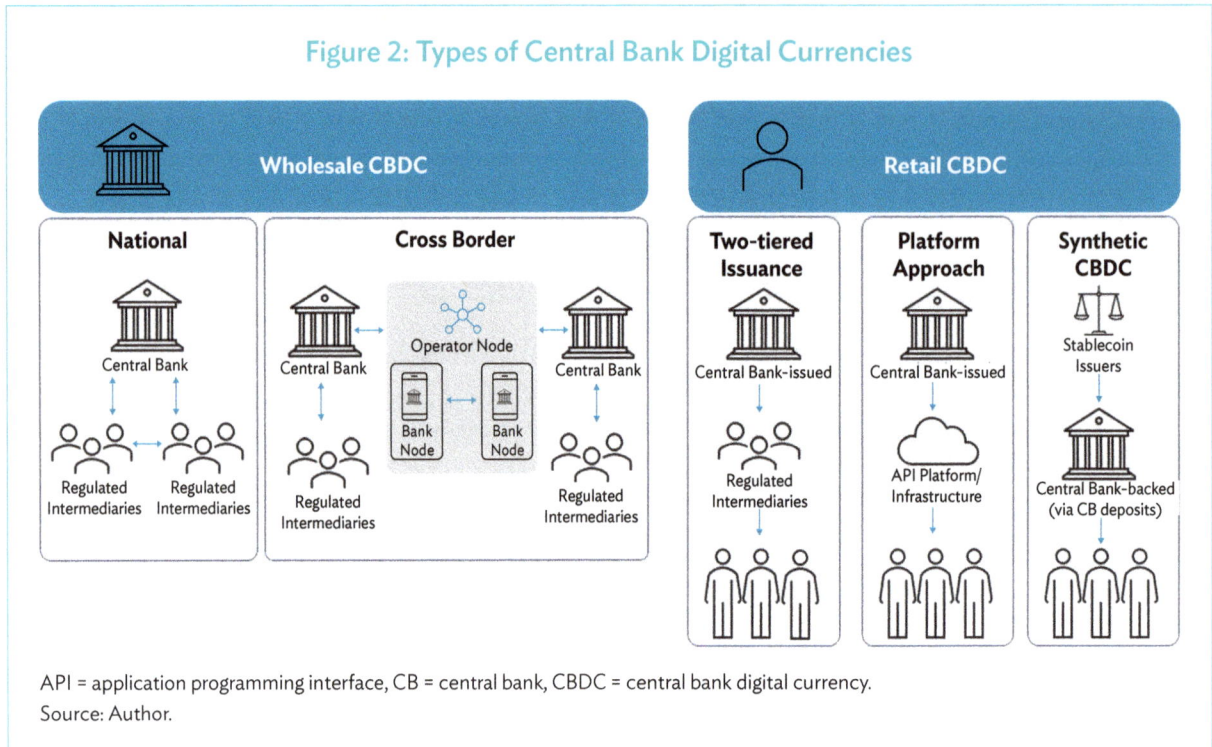

Figure 2: Types of Central Bank Digital Currencies

API = application programming interface, CB = central bank, CBDC = central bank digital currency.
Source: Author.

of central-bank-authorized digital currency must be matched with a local or appropriate foreign currency, and it is slower to increase supply (BIS 2020a). The advantage of central-bank-authorized digital currency is that those payment companies other than banks can be part of a new payment system (Coindesk 2021), usually through DLT, rather than settling the trades through the traditional RTGS or automated clearing house. This model suggests that it can provide the capability for central banks to better control the speed and flow of central-bank-authorized digital currency, especially in cross-country transactions or remittances. A hybrid, also known as general-purpose CBDC, is defined as one that is made available to both wholesale and retail counterparts.

Among wholesale CBDCs, projects initiated by Canada; Hong Kong, China; Singapore; and Thailand aim to address issues related to cross-border settlement.

Peer-to-Peer Transactions or through Intermediaries

CBDCs can have both P2P transactions and transactions through intermediaries. P2P transactions refer to two parties sending and receiving digital currency or assets without a third party or any intermediaries.

An advantage of P2P transactions, and the adoption of cryptography or DLT, is that it allows safe offline token-based CBDC transfer, which is difficult in traditional account-based transactions since validating the account holder's identity and account balance under the system are the prerequisite for a transaction to occur.

In both P2P and transactions through intermediaries, it is possible to have shielded transactions (MAS 2017),[31] as experimented in Project Ubin for the latter. It is also possible to transfer token-based CBDC safely offline, whereas account-based transactions cannot occur without validating the account holder's identity and its account balance under the system.

Discussions on token-based versus account-based CBDCs have been covered extensively by the IMF (2018, 2020b), BIS (2020c), Bank of Canada (2018), and others. The authors of these papers note that an account-based system requires verification of payee and payer identities, while a token-based system requires verifying the validity of the object used to pay. The account-based design has to verify the payer's identity and balance. Access to the fund depends on the accounts, or in other words, the identities. Losing passwords or private keys will not affect fund transfer. As long as a person can prove his or her identity to the centralized authority maintaining the account, the passwords can be retrieved or re-issued. Under the token-based CBDC, the token's authenticity is verified just as the physical currency, e.g., through the possession of a private cryptographic key. The main point is that, technically, one's identity is not needed if there is a private key to prove ownership, and with verification via digital signature,[32] the currency can be sent from the payer to the payee. This distinction causes much confusion. The other way to look at the issue is custody- versus non-custody-based CBDCs.

Losing the private key is equivalent to losing the tokens, or, in the physical sense, losing cash in physical wallets. Indeed, token transactions need not have an account or be customized, but it does not mean that they cannot involve an account managed or customized by a third party such as a crypto bank, a payment service provider, or a virtual asset service provider.[33]

Direct or Two-Tier Models

A direct model refers to a one-tier CBDC for which the central bank issues and performs payment and circulation functions. A synthetic CBDC or central-bank-authorized digital currency is a representative form of the two-tier system, whereby the central-bank-authorized CBDC is issued by a commercial bank and fully backed with domestic or foreign central bank liabilities or other forms of reserves. One-tier is when the central bank creates

---

[31] Corda workstreams, Hyperledger Fabric, and Quorum designs use different cryptography techniques involving public key infrastructure, bilateral channel, smart contracts, and zero-knowledge proofs to achieve privacy in fund transfer functionality. Identities may be known only to the user and not others with public key infrastructure, the bilateral channel is only transparent to the two transacting parties, and private smart contracts between two parties with verification via zero-knowledge proofs to shield the transactions.

[32] A digital signature is a mathematical scheme for verifying the authenticity of digital messages or documents and, in the case of a CBDC, the possession of a private key that allows the transfer of the digital currency. Digital signature is different from an electronic signature as the latter is the digital representation of a signature, while the former is a mathematical proof that a user is in possession of the private key. For those not familiar with the private key, it is an easy-to-use authentication tool such as biometric identification that can be used to trigger the transfer via a private key embedded in the hardware e-wallet. CBDC, residing on such a payment system, may use a set of cryptographic keys that allow easy transfer between parties without a formal banking account. Depending on the amount transacted, regulators may use tiered-KYC to request more information from individuals as the amount increases.

[33] A virtual asset service provider means any natural or legal person not covered elsewhere under the Financial Action Task Force recommendations, and as a business conduct one or more of the following activities or operations for or on behalf of another natural or legal person:

  i.   exchange between virtual assets and fiat currencies;

  ii. exchange between one or more forms of virtual assets;

  iii. transfer (in this context of virtual assets, transfer means to conduct a transaction on behalf of another natural or legal person that moves a virtual asset from one virtual asset address or account to another) of virtual assets;

  iv. safekeeping and/or administration of virtual assets or instruments enabling control over virtual assets; and

  v.   participation in and provision of financial services related to an issuer's offer and/or sale of a virtual asset.

  See Financial Action Task Force Recommendations at https://www.fatf-gafi.org/glossary/u-z/ for information.

the currency, while the two-tier model is when the intermediaries issue the note backed by fiat or other central bank liabilities or other reserves.

A hybrid model is one with a direct claim on the central bank, with both intermediaries or an agency handling payment and other administrative functions. A token-based CBDC accessible on a central bank e-wallet has sovereign risk, while a token-based CBDC (or its private key) on a commercial bank's ledger contains both corporate and sovereign risk. The two-tier model has two advantages: (i) it can transfer counterparty risk liabilities to a regulated intermediary to avoid a bank run, and (ii) it can alleviate the shock of removing intermediatory institutions in the financial sector.

It is also possible to have a CBDC (or its private key) stored/in custody at other central banks' approved agents, including a central bank agent, payment companies, or licensed e-wallet providers, instead of commercial banks. In still other examples, these tokens are decentralized and reside on a DLT or a blockchain that requires banks or agencies to manage the private key rather than a deposit. An added advantage is that no liquidity pool or reserves are needed for the DLT-based central-bank-authorized digital currency, thus lowering entry barriers for non bank licensed payment services providers and settlement costs.

Unspent Transaction Output versus State-Based Model

Two concepts from cryptocurrency are used in the design of a CBDC: unspent transaction output (UTXO) general ledger and local state-based ledger. One either tracks the transactions in a general ledger or captures the local state or account of the ledgers. To track the payments, UTXO and code-based methods (the codes are captured in the local state or the specific account) are used in a CBDC. These concepts of UTXO or the state-based model are important in understanding the opportunities and risks of CBDCs. In particular, UTXO is similar to a messaging system and considered relatively secure in P2P transactions. The state-based model is similar to one simply capturing the balance of an account at a particular time or state. This is useful if smart contracts are to be used, because the ledger can reflect the state of the smart contracts, especially before and after they are executed. Both these designs present different opportunities and suffer from different types of risks.

There are no accounts or a record for the user balance in an UTXO-based ledger, only a general state of the ledger consisting of outputs, spent and unspent. Coins are stored as a list of unspent transaction outputs or spent transaction outputs (STXO).[34] Each UTXO has a quantity and criteria for spending it. Existing UTXO (denoted by Y) has to be spent completely. Once spent, Y is removed from the pool. If X is to be spent, the balance (Y-X) will be received by the sender as a change. Both X and (Y-X) are the UTXOs, while Y is marked as a non-unspent transaction output or STXO. Transactions are created by consuming existing UTXOs and producing UTXOs in their place (Clifford 2019). An UTXO is akin to a list of coins that gets transferred by satisfying the current spending criteria and can be divided or combined to create the denomination needed for a particular transaction. The PBOC uses this UTXO method to keep track of every transaction of e-CNY.

---

[34] In cryptocurrency definitions, coins are native to (or generated by) the distributed ledger, while tokens do not have their own distributed ledger but are created or issued with a smart contract. This paper follows the definition of the Inland Revenue Authority of Singapore that cryptocurrencies are considered digital payment tokens: see https://www.iras.gov.sg/irashome/GST/GST-registered-businesses/Specific-business-sectors/Digital-Payment-Tokens/.

An account or local state-based ledger can capture the balance of the CBDC user account at any state.[35] It not only captures the coins' transactions, but it can also capture the state of the computer codes or the smart contracts. Instead of having each coin uniquely referenced, coins are represented as a balance within an account. Accounts can either be controlled by a private key or a smart contract. The distributed ledger may contain information at a particular account or local state at a particular time.[36] This information may include the balance of anything of value, such as a CBDC, the associated codes, and any other data content. A private key is needed to spend the coins and move the computer codes or execute the smart contracts from one state to another. This is not to be confused with the "centralized account-based" model that can be accessed by a password that is controlled by the administrator. However, a UTXO model is consistent with a centralized account-based model. Suppose an administrator holds the private keys, the administrator can issue a password, and the users will be able to access the service provider's e-wallet via a password.

For example, Hyperledger Iroha can create and manage simple digital assets like a CBDC, or complex ones like identity, indivisible rights, certificate authenticity, and patents. Cambodia's Project Bakong[37] is a blockchain-based central-bank-authorized digital currency using the Hyperledger Iroha blockchain (National Bank of Cambodia 2020, Palanivel 2018). Bakong uses the state-based account balance approach with Hyperledger Iroha, and Project Ubin experimented with various distributed ledgers, with one version of the Digital Singapore dollar on an Ethereum private blockchain. MAS's Ethereum was designed to be compatible with current account-based systems and the RTGS systems and allows for a working integrated transfer prototype to facilitate payment versus payment and delivery versus payment.

In summary, a CBDC is usually issued and monitored by a country's central bank,[38] and it is not without centralized or decentralized control like Bitcoin (BIS 2018b). A blockchain-based token can be an independent form of a digital representation of a country's fiat currency (European Parliament 2019). Among the many categorizations, one is to base it on user accessibility. For example, a wholesale CBDC is only accessible to a specific number of firms, whereas the retail CBDC is widely available to consumers (Auer, Cornelli, and Frost 2020).

CBDC designs can incorporate or combine any of the features above for specific purposes, e.g., P2P two-tier with state-based ledger, P2P direct with unspent transaction output, or P2P through intermediary with two-tier state-based model, among other combinations. An efficient e-payment tool may fulfill the objective for financial inclusion, e.g., the cryptographic key is used for easy transfer offline among unknown parties for smaller amounts, and these UTXOs or state-based distributed systems may be used to capture the entire transaction record. When retail CBDC is associated with "digitization" or "tokenization" with a pair of cryptographic keys and able to transact P2P, even when offline, the advantages of the "cash-like" feature are apparent. Data are captured with privacy protection for smaller amounts. While the CBDC may resemble cash, traceability is an added advantage that cash does not offer.

Finally, more innovative models and new definitions of CBDCs may emerge, as they are still in the early stages of development. This report is a compilation and a presentation of a framework, but it is not exhaustive.

---

35   In a distributed system, the local state may consist of only those records that form part of the database and excludes temporary records used in computation. The global state of a distributed system is the set of local states of each individual processes involved in the system plus the state of the communication channels.

36   Absolute or clock time is not as crucial as knowing the order in which events occurred in a distributed system. Time can be measured or viewed as in "block," and each block information is a state and may take a different time to form.

37   According to the central banks of Cambodia and the PRC, their digital currencies are authorized but not issued by the central banks. Therefore, the digital currency is not a liability on the central bank's balance sheet but resembles the currency board system.

38   Theoretically, central-bank-authorized digital currencies can be issued by either corporates or central banks, or both.

3 Opportunities and Risks of Central Bank Digital Currencies

Opportunities

Opportunities fall under two different areas:

(i) For developing countries in Asia and the Pacific, a CBDC may help improve financial inclusion.
(ii) For advanced economies, an appropriately designed CBDC may help improve cross-border payment and settlement efficiency.

By fostering digitalization, appropriate designs may address big techs' market/data dominance and concentration, as well as data and privacy protection. Emerging opportunities arising from CBDCs include improvements in convenience, inclusion, risk mitigation, accurate measurement of economic activity, monetary and fiscal sovereignty, managed anonymity, elimination or lowering of trusted third-party cost for inclusion, more statistics on financial inclusion, innovation, distribution, and more clarity in lending.

(i) Convenience

A CBDC can be designed for P2P transactions while online and offline. The design of a CBDC has the potential to overcome the challenge of offline P2P transactions by eliminating intermediaries or without a third-party system. Whether it is a centralized system with UTXO or a DLT system, the data are updated when the devices containing the P2P transactions information are back online. Near-field-communication-enabled, or other offline hardware wallet technology lessens the reliance on the internet/mobile network and reduces the risk of disruption of services while offline. CBDCs designed for offline transactions bring the same convenience as physical cash.

(ii) Inclusion

The design of CBDCs permits more general P2P value transfer via e-wallets without the need for a formal bank account, or any link to financial institutions or cards for e-money. A private system can do the same, but central-bank-authorized digital currency can bypass the traditional RTGS and automated clearing house. A simple download of application software can replace the complicated, inconvenient, and costly onboarding process for users at the most basic level. A CBDC can then function similar to physical transactions using cash. It eliminates the intermediary and counterparty risk. The breakdown in trust among licensed payment institutions during crises is a bottleneck for central banks' efforts to distribute money to the ultimate beneficiaries. A central-bank-authorized digital currency with DLT has the potential to lower the cost of entry by eliminating or minimizing counterparty risk.

(iii) Risk mitigation

A CBDC may improve a payment system's efficiency and security without going through a clearing house or RTGS, while retaining monetary sovereignty. This bypassing of a trusted third party mitigates the risk of a breakdown or an attack on any bank's or third party's centralized system or clearing house system. If it is a blockchain-based CBDC, DLT allows avoidance of a single point of failure.

(iv) Accurate economic activity measurement

CBDCs may facilitate more accurate representation of economic activities that are currently excluded from national accounting. Many small transactions occur without going through the banking or financial system, but they are essential economic activities. A retail CBDC may capture payments associated with primary activities that are currently not reflected in the national accounts.

(v) Monetary and fiscal sovereignty

CBDCs offer the potential to ward off the challenge of non-fiat e-money replacing fiat money, so as to prevent the loss of monetary and fiscal policy sovereignty. There is a danger that a more liquid or convenient form of foreign CBDC may affect the velocity of local currency and thus monetary policy. With e-money and e-commerce, payments using other alternative currencies may lower tax revenue as traceability may be an issue for the tax authority when the goods and services traded are in digital form on the borderless virtual space. However, an inclusive distributed payment system that accommodates more payment companies may reduce the incentives and opportunities of tax evasion. A less-inclusive CBDC payment system relative to the alternatives may worsen the situation, especially if the CBDC is accessible only to a small group and fails to capture essential transaction data.

(vi) Managed anonymity

Privacy refers to keeping the activities of an individual online hidden even though everyone knows their identity. Anonymity keeps the identity hidden, even though the activities are visible to everyone. CBDCs can build in a capability to maintain privacy and/or anonymity while preventing money laundering, terrorist financing, tax evasion, and criminal activities.

Managed anonymity refers to the amount of information or data collected on the individual, either keeping the activities of the individual hidden from institutions or government, or simply not collecting the data at all. Managed anonymity also refers to keeping the identity of users partially hidden or simply not collecting it. The government can prescribe the amount of information to be collected by licensed institutions based on materiality. For example, the central authority obtains full information only if the individual agrees or that an amount or that the frequency of transactions has exceeded a threshold. AI and data analytics can identify patterns of money laundering and other illegal activities, as a CBDC is more transparent than cash.

Introducing a tiered system for CBDC onboarding suggests some advantages. At the most basic level, an individual may download the app and even receive small payments or x number of transactions from anywhere globally without revealing any personal information but a phone number.[39] To send or spend a small amount of the CBDC, some basic identification information of the individual or tourist (such as the phone number) may

---

[39] "The least-privileged wallets can be opened without providing identities to reflect the principle of anonymity. Users can open least-privileged anonymous wallets by default and upgrade them to higher-level, real-name ones as needed." (PBOC 2021).

have to be uploaded. Alipay and WeChat Pay have similar arrangements. This tiered approach reduces the cost of onboarding. It increases social scalability beyond the country of issue and for short-term tourists. It has proven to be useful for tax rebates from other countries for visits to foreign countries. The higher second tier that allows for a larger amount of transactions and storage requires opening a bank account, linking to a phone number, or linking with a credit or debit card. The third tier requires physical presence for identification at a designated licensed entity. It is debatable whether such private information should be in the hands of the private enterprises or the government. A CBDC can empower the central bank in big data analysis and, at the same time, lessen the control and privacy invasion of the financial institutions with managed anonymity guidelines. CBDCs lower the enforcement costs of private enterprises, especially if the government controls the industry standards of an e-wallet with its own CBDC digital infrastructure.

(vii) Elimination or lowering of trusted third-party cost for inclusion

CBDCs allow the incorporation of digital or smart contracts, as in the e-CNY of the PRC's DCEP project, and Project Ubin for payment versus payment and delivery versus payment. Digital agreements are useful when trusted third parties are needed. When the transactions are small, the cost of these trusted third-party digital contracts may be higher than the contract value. Decentralized digital enforcement codes (more commonly known as smart contracts) can be executed automatically without a trusted third-party. Smart contracts reduce third-party trust but may not necessarily eliminate a trusted third party. New forms of trusted third parties may evolve but they will likely have a lower cost of trust than the current form. When the cost is lower than the contract value of the transaction, a new class of lower-value transactions is now viable. This innovation from DLT CBDCs has implications for many areas with imperfect justice systems and weak enforcement environments for legal agreements, as smart contracts may address the pain point of nonperformance of a deal and stimulate investment.

(viii) More statistics on financial inclusion

More complete data on transactions can help indicate ways to stimulate growth in the underserved, under-recorded, and under represented sectors. Gross domestic product national accounts do not capture many low-traded, minute transactions, illiquid assets, and unrecorded economic activities. Tokenization tracks household services, livestock trading, and many other unrecorded and unreported activities. Informal sector actors are motivated to use cash because of tax evasion. Many countries struggle to increase access to financial accounts because small business owners are reluctant to pay taxes on their sales. These market participants may continue to use cash unless it becomes very inconvenient, or the customers or the counterparty require them to do so. If a CBDC is convenient and becomes a preferred medium of payment, activities may be captured. Capturing the excluded economic events in the national accounts leads to better policy making for sustainable growth. These essential and omitted statistics of primary economic activities in aggregation can be substantial in agriculture, especially in less-developed economies.

The key is to retain the desirable characteristics of cash, manage anonymity, make it easy to use, keep it secure, and balance the need for enforcement for illegal activities. Another potential benefit of CBDCs is to capture those excluded essential economic activities and devise a better sustainable growth policy.[40]

---

[40]   Such as household activities, volunteer services, preservation of ecosystem, informal lending, gaming activities, online activities, tax evasion, and other shadow economy activities. Smart contracts (for transaction) and decentralized finance (for price discovery) provide avenues and incentives for such activities to be recorded.

(ix) Innovation driver

If designed appropriately, CBDCs support innovation in payments and future payment needs in a digital economy.[41] The potential benefits vary according to design. Allowing a flexible second tier to innovate may reap maximum benefits for central banks. CBDCs may involve public-private partnerships, which may give rise to a more secure and resilient payment system, with continual improvements and keeping up to date with technological improvements. Becoming a favorable digital currency jurisdiction and creating an attractive ecosystem could lead to enhanced economic activity but could also create spillover effects in other technology sectors. With DLT and smart contracts, the cost of trust is reduced and thus may increase industry collaboration activities, reaping the digital economy's network effect. The two-tier design that allows for innovation at the second tier with the principle of subsidiarity[42] may create new business models, reduce friction for payments, lower business costs, and empower small and medium-sized enterprises to innovate with e-wallet facilities. Those new activities give rise to new business models with new jobs, provided that regulation is in line with innovation, not front-running or lagging behind innovation.

(x) Distribution

This allows a government to provide short-term liquidity assistance directly to the needy with certainty. CBDCs could enhance payment system competition and efficiency, and lower barriers to entry of innovative players,[43] and increase resilience in the face of greater concentration in the hands of a few giant companies. Payment systems may become natural monopolies, reflecting strong network externalities, economies of scale, and economies of scope. However, some private money issuers may not internalize the social cost of possible systemic disruptions from operational failure, including cyberattacks, and thus may underinvest in security. Monopolistic private issuers may also abuse that power, leading to inefficiency, by offering partial, inadequate, and expensive services. They could also commercialize collected user data, although these could also invite competition, depending on entry barriers. These arguments might justify CBDC issuance or some jurisdictions' decisions to deploy fast payment systems, giving them control over an essential piece of the payment architecture. In the e-CNY design, the second tier CBDC model can extend beyond the banks and include retail outlets in providing the e-wallets to retail customers. These will encourage competition for payment services.

(xi) More clarity on currency in circulation

Policy makers may know the maximum amount of the money supply based on an increase in the banking system's reserves and loan reporting without a CBDC. However, the willingness to lend is unpredictable, and so is the resulting loan amount. Possible real-time traceability of CBDCs could lead to more transparency and real-time available data for policy makers.

---

[41] Debate is ongoing about what design is allowed in the second tier in the DCEP (Equalocean 2020).

[42] Subsidiarity is a principle of social organization that holds that social and political issues should be dealt with at the most immediate level consistent with their resolution. Any action by the higher authority should not go beyond what is necessary to achieve the objectives and should, as far as possible, delegate the authority to the next lower level.

[43] The introduction of CBDCs can be expected to prevent certain private payment companies including credit cards, prepaid cards, and big techs from monopolizing the payment system of one country as the number of payment instruments that people can use with cash increases. In other words, small-scale offline merchants and e-commerce companies could be prevented from being subject to a particular payment company.

Risks

Bank runs can happen when trust is lost in a banking system. And how a central bank ensures consumers and firms trust the banks is a fundamental issue. Once financial institutions lose trust during a "run," such as on banks, it affects stability, with a heavy economic price to pay. The design of a CBDC is particularly important, calling for clear understanding of how it can impact on the existing monetary system's confidence when it is introduced. For example, the introduction of CBDCs might alienate segments of the population such as the poor or old people with insufficient digital infrastructure access or required skills.

CBDC risks include bank runs; risks of financial disintermediation of incumbents; technical and security risks; legal and supervision risks; currency circulation risks resulting in exclusion; emergence of CBDC derivatives and engineered products; attracting valuation premium during crises; uncertainty surrounding design and monetary policy management; loss of convenience with custody of private keys, fake wallets; and financial exclusion.

(i)   Risks of bank runs

With CBDCs, bank runs in financial crises are potentially faster and independent of geographical proximity and time. Assuming that there are no limits to transfers between bank deposits and CBDCs, there are risks of bank runs. During a crisis, the switch from bank deposits to CBDCs to avoid the third-party risk of financial intermediaries may be more severe and intense than the traditional withdrawal methods.

(ii)   Risks of financial disintermediation of incumbents

Even though the consensus is to design CBDCs without interest, for exploratory purposes and completeness, it may still be relevant to discuss positive and negative interest rates on CBDCs. Interest-bearing central-bank-issued digital currency may be a close substitute for bank deposits. Its introduction may crowd out bank deposits or a rise in deposit rates, and motivate banks to shift from deposit funding to wholesale funding. In central-bank-authorized digital currency, even though it is authorized but not issued by the central bank, there must be confidence in the central bank to strictly uphold the "currency board" rules. The legacy issues and costs may slow incumbents' innovation relative to the new asset-light fintech players, which are nimbler. Thus, CBDCs may expose the inefficiency of some incumbents. This transition from an asset-heavy to an asset-light e-wallet-focused financial industry may be riskier to developed markets than in developing markets in Asia. Asia, especially if the financial sector is small relative to other sectors, may take a more relaxed and experimental approach given its lower systematic risk. It is still too early to draw any conclusion if the transition risk is more considerable than expected. CBDCs may also bear negative interest rates such that holding on to the CBDC may be costly. The level of negative interest to prevent hoarding and acting as a risk-free store of value asset class for international fund managers is an area for research. For an open economy, capital flows and exchange rates are sensitive to a change in interest rate and it is unclear what impact a negative nominal interest rate would have.

(iii)   Technical and security risk

CBDCs may be vulnerable to power outages, poor connection, and technology risk, especially from the technical design. However, many such technologies are still in the early stage of development, and there are problems such as inconsistent technical standards and insufficient technical scalability that need to be resolved before their large-scale adoption. From the perspective of a transaction, CBDCs solve account book tampering and reversibility problems, but may not solve personal information security. If hackers attack the user's private key, property loss may occur. When a CBDC is a token, there may not be recourse when lost or stolen. The cost of having a trusted third party to safeguard the private key may also incur additional costs. Sophisticated and mature cybersecurity capabilities are needed, and skilling up for central banks and service providers is essential. One main challenge for many existing licensed institutions is that very few sophisticated risk teams and operation rooms monitor every transaction of the e-wallets. The lack of such high-intensity monitoring to prevent fraud and crimes is due to privacy protection issues. More sophisticated cryptography methods of tracing while protecting privacy would likely be the focus in the future, while security issues remain a challenge.

(iv)   Legal and supervision risk

Central banks in many countries have legal gaps in issuance, use, circulation, and digital currency supervision, such as in the treatment of deposit insurance for CBDCs. There are also challenges in monitoring and supervising CBDCs.

For example, in traditional currency supervision, banks can detect physical counterfeits and withdraw them from the system. However, digital currency does not exist in physical form but is accessible from a software and hardware e-wallet. Its counterfeiting and supervision methods are different. The loss can be massive and widespread if there is a software bug. The security issue may be more severe than traditional currency when hackers steal or when a system failure occurs.

(v)   Currency circulation risks with inadequate open digital infrastructure

The circulation of CBDCs is closely related to internet infrastructure and telecom operators. Although smartphones are popular, many people are still excluded from the financial system. The network infrastructure in some areas may be poor. The penetration rate of smartphones may be low, which affects the adoption of CBDCs. Moreover, poor public digital literacy about CBDC custody technology may lead to the loss of private keys and digital currency scams.

In the PRC, much effort has gone into ensuring that digitalization initiatives benefit many people (financial inclusion) and corporates (corporate inclusion). The design of the e-CNY aims to ensure that few citizens are left out and allow capable corporates beyond banks to be involved in the DCEP (Ledger Insights 2021). The Postal Savings Bank of China is the first commercial bank to introduce a digital yuan biometric hardware wallet. The wallet, which resembles a debit card, comes with a small display that shows all payment details and balance information and the fund is secured by an engraved Norwegian IDEX Biometrics fingerprint sensor (Wang 2021). There are also efforts to have a risk-based method of inclusion to reduce compliance with full KYC. The PRC's DCEP wallets could be offered in the future in a multi-tier (four- or five-tier) system, which would potentially cap how much users can spend of their digital yuan and manage their anonymity according to the amount and frequency of use. The smaller and the less frequent the e-wallet is used, the less stringent the KYC process. The idea would be similar to an actual wallet that stores physical cash, with one key difference. DCEP hardware wallets can be traceable and strip away the anonymity of paper cash, as users would need personal information such as IDs and phone numbers to activate the wallet when a certain threshold is triggered (Zhao 2020). In this case, more users can be included with lower compliance costs, especially if the user's amount is small and infrequent. Unless a country pays enough attention to user inclusion and literacy, there is a severe risk of exclusion due to the lack of open, user-friendly, affordable open digital infrastructure.

(vi)   Emergence of CBDC derivatives and engineered products

Financial market policy transmission mechanisms and infrastructure interactions are complex. There are uncertainties and risks in engineered products of CBDCs because of the speed and intensity of transactions and the volume involved. Policy makers need to pay attention to these derivatives when promoting digital currency pilots. For example, the PRC has a regulation to prohibit the tokenization of renminbi and has initiated a new cryptography law. It is challenging, however, for many regulators to monitor the derivatives markets, which, with smart contracts, can mushroom in a compressed time frame.

(vii) Attracting valuation premium during crises

If the supply of a CBDC is fixed with interest payments, there may be a valuation premium in times of a rush to safety. There is a need for a stabilizing mechanism to prevent a mismatch between demand and supply. Even if a stabilizing mechanism can be autonomous with smart contracts, the learning curve for most regulators remains steep. Decentralized finance can help, but the acquisition of education and experience takes time.

(viii) Uncertainty surrounding design and monetary policy management

Doubts about the choice of design and blind spots of new technology may lead to uncertainties. For example, the determinants of demand for money and interest rates affect the transmission of monetary policy. The market may react unpredictably during the transition period, and the loss of trust may have contagion effects. Furthermore, the increase in liabilities in the central bank balance sheet may affect investment demand in government securities and commercial bank loans, and thus cause fluctuations in foreign reserves and increase the volatility of exchange rates. A subsequent divestment may cause volatility in less-developed and thinly traded capital and debt markets, triggering a crisis.

(ix) Loss of convenience with custody for private keys, and fake wallets

If a CBDC as a token requires a private key or a specialized wallet, there are dangers, as the user may fall victim to hacks or fraud through their own actions or bugs in the code of wallet or fake wallets. If CBDCs are limited to storing at approved institutions, there is a trade-off between security and convenience. In fact, by appointing a custodian for the private keys, there may not be full control of the CBDC by the individual. Limiting the use of third-party providers may defeat the purpose of issuing a CBDC for convenience and availability.

(x) Financial exclusion

With the lack of digital literacy, basic understanding of financial instruments, and inability to trust technology, segments of the population may be excluded or alienated, such as poor people and old people, who lack access to digital infrastructure. There is some importance in establishing open public digital financial infrastructure, without which more people will be excluded than included.

Another risk exists here, related to the issue of digital and financial literacy. Digital and financial or simply fintech illiteracy may result in exclusion. In that sense, a CBDC may have negative impact on the economy and society. These exclusion risks may be alleviated by building digital infrastructure, improving digital literacy of the vulnerable population, and empowering the small businesses through CBDC education programs.

Many of these risks may be managed via appropriate CBDC designs and definitions. For example, if a CBDC is not part of M1/M2, meaning that it is M0 (monetary base). CBDCs are not competing with deposits and that policy risk is taken care of by the money definitions under the CDBC: appropriate definitions and designs provide useful policy implications. In addition, building digital infrastructure supports financial inclusion and education empowers the people and enterprises when a CBDC is introduced.

In summary, while there is more consensus now that a CBDC is a public good and may not bear interest, any discussion is conditional on the feasible CBDC designs and models in development. Every country will take a different path. Even within a country, it is risky for the central bank to single out a so-called optimal technology roadmap, and anti-competition regulations are required to clear hurdles for technology innovation. The central banks' research and development will likely focus on a secure and reliable settlement and clearing infrastructure in conjunction with digital currency. New designs and new models will mitigate many of the abovementioned risks and may introduce new ones. Theoretically, a CBDC can bear interest if regulation allows. New CBDC classification may emerge in the future, e.g., a new classification other than M0 or M1. There will inevitably be new definitions, laws, legislation, and regulations. The discussions here are on current CBDC developments, and many of these risks may disappear and others emerge as governments gain better understanding and respond accordingly with new measures.

4 Recent Developments in Central Bank Digital Currencies in Asia

In 2019, representing 62 of the world's central banks, the BIS reported that 70% of its members were researching the potential effects of CBDCs on their economies (Boar, Holden, and Wadsworth 2020). The paradigm shift of the COVID-19 pandemic and the threat from stablecoins have accelerated central bank interest in CBDC exploration (Falempin 2020). By November 2020, 80% of central banks were investigating CBDCs (Boar and Wehrli 2021). In global retail CBDC developments, as of this writing, two CBDC projects had been fully launched (the Bahamas and Cambodia), three had completed their pilots (Ecuador, Ukraine, and Uruguay), and six were at an advanced stage pilot or proof of concept (Auer, Cornelli, and Frost 2020). Although dynamic CBDC development trackers are available,[44] they do not accurately portray developments.[45]

CBDC money is distinguished from other forms of digital money by its token-type unit of account, whereby claims are honored based solely on demonstrated knowledge, such as a digital signature (Auer and Böhme 2020b). The possibility of tokenized currency with smart contracts for autonomous real-time settlement 24 hours, 7 days a week is an attractive proposition.

In Asia, central banks and monetary authorities are releasing research, proofs of concept, and implementation. The Bank of Thailand launched a pilot in June 2020; the Bank of Korea announced plans for a 2021 CBDC pilot; Japan articulated a passive course of interest; and Cambodia; the PRC; Hong Kong, China; Singapore; and Thailand are taking the lead.

Smaller nations have different objectives, but the financial experimentation made possible by the smaller national banking systems makes them more agile and more autonomous. Small size means the global dependence on their currency is smaller and changing course with nascent technology less costly.

Further, successful interoperability will bring rewards. Some economies, such as Saudi Arabia and the United Arab Emirates, show more significant interest, especially economies with greater autonomy, low debt, natural reserves, and international trade. Phase 2 of the Project Inthanon-LionRock project (Hong Kong, China; Thailand) involves five entities for cross-border transfer of value. This project, supported by the BIS Innovation Hub, plans to gauge the feasibility of more efficient cross-border payments. With CBDC projects, each economy explores interoperability and pilot tests to facilitate all settlements and cross-border payment concerns. The G20, Financial Stability Board, and BIS have made notable efforts in enhancing cross-border payments (FSB 2020).

In addition to cross-border projects, the two-tier model is also emerging as an exciting proposition. Cambodia tackles financial inclusion via a dual access model of either (i) an account claim via a two-tier KYC system to allow excluded users to leverage an intermediatory payment hub mechanism, or (ii) a token claim via direct wallet

---

[44]   The most frequently visited CBDC tracker sites include https://cbdctracker.org/ and https://cbdc.bohem.tech/.
[45]   Appendix 5 Global Central Bank Digital Currency Developments.

usage. Since the riel or the US dollar fully backs the token, it functions like coins and notes in a physical wallet, lowering the service costs through payment companies, in that it eliminates counterparty risk.

More innovative models have been surfacing in Asia, with the lack of cheap technology and some economies partial exclusion from the international payment system encouraging them to become first movers. Projects in developed economies, such as the US and Japan, remain preliminary and wholesale focused.

The most advanced CBDC retail projects' models are based on their design in (i) architecture, (ii) infrastructure, (iii) access, and (iv) interoperability of cross-border capabilities.[46] Apart from the retail-focused objective of financial inclusion, cross-border payment efficiency using CBDCs is a noted common interest (CPMI 2020) for bilateral and now multilateral experiments (the ECB and BOJ in 2019, PBOC and MAS in 2019, and Bank of Thailand and HKMA in 2020).

The key motivation for wholesale CBDC utility is to explore improved efficiency of payment versus payment, and delivery versus payment of cross-border payments to reduce settlement risks (i.e., by settling directly with central bank liabilities) provided 24/7, widen interoperability with other settlement systems, and to reduce turnaround time significantly.[47]

It has also become clear that the success of the CBDC is dependent on interoperability. CBDCs aim to facilitate cross-border transactions through seamless and inexpensive payments, given demand from international trade and e-commerce, remittances, and tourism. A CBDC design will therefore incorporate interlinkage options to facilitate cross-border activity from the start (Bech, Faruqui, and Shirakami 2020).

However, regulatory risks and barriers are still very prevalent due to global compliance disparity. Although DLT may remove the barrier to membership of counterparty systems at a basic technical level, foresight on addressing business arrangements still poses a challenge (Auer, Haene, and Holden 2021).

---

[46]   Refer to Appendix 5 and Table 1 for CBDC design factors.
[47]   Appendixes 5 and 6 summarizes globally notable retail and wholesale CBDC projects.

5 Objectives, Motivations, and Considerations

Objectives and Motivations

One of the basic objectives of a central bank is to provide trust in money as a public good to facilitate financial transactions. However, the world is constantly transforming with new technology, and so is money and the role of central banks. While the motivation is to provide cash as a means of payment, a CBDC may complement central bank money to the public, supporting a more resilient and diverse domestic payment system, as well as offering opportunities not possible with cash while supporting innovation (BIS 2020a). The timing of issuance and the underlying design of CBDC are considerations for central banks once a decision to launch is reached.

CBDCs will enhance efficiency in payments and settlement. They may also facilitate payment versus payment and the settlement of digital assets using smart contracts. More importantly, CBDCs may help address issues of data and privacy protection, as well as data ownership issues associated with the rent-seeking behavior of fintech or bigtech monopolies in more-developed economies. These are the main focus of developed economies. Financial inclusion, on the other hand, is one of the main reasons for the introduction of CBDCs and the concept of inclusion has expanded beyond individuals to include corporates such as payment companies that are very innovative. Besides promoting efficiency and innovation, there are other objectives such as financial stability and the complementary function of CBDCs to existing money and payment functions. For developing economies, the priorities may well be different and may include improving payment system resilience and competition, facilitating cross-border transactions, as well as increasing financial inclusion and improving social protection initiatives.

Important for launching a CBDC are informed judgment about these risks, the potential effects on market structure, the implications for financial stability, and safeguards incorporated in the design of the CBDC.

The choice of currency type designed for wholesale or retail is also dynamic. Although the degree of balance among the objectives may vary, the PRC's intention of balancing the objectives is highlighted, as it may be relevant for developing economies. Specifically, the PRC's central bank has addressed inclusion and efficiency objectives[48] with its two-tier issuance model (Mitsui & Co. 2020).

---

[48] PBOC Deputy Governor Fan Yifei was quoted by *Beijing News* as focusing on supervision. There was a lack of transparency or ability for the central bank to supervise payment companies, which was rectified. The central bank was unable to determine to which individual the transaction related in the Omnibus Account of the payment companies. Another issue relates to interoperability, as users cannot scan each other's codes across platforms, but DCEP wallets will be compatible with each other. See *Ledger Insights* (2020).

Design Considerations

We present a general framework for a CBDC that includes many designs of CBDC (Figure 3):

- Layer 1 decision: The issuance of a CBDC.
- Layer 2 decision: The core-satellite payment system that links the user.
- Layer 3 decision: The authentication, registration, and query functions.

There are two-tier considerations for a CBDC: the first is the approach to currency issuance, i.e., how the digital currency will be issued. The second is the payment methods among wholesale and retail banking. The central bank can centralize the decision for the approaches or relax control of payments once the digital currency is in circulation.

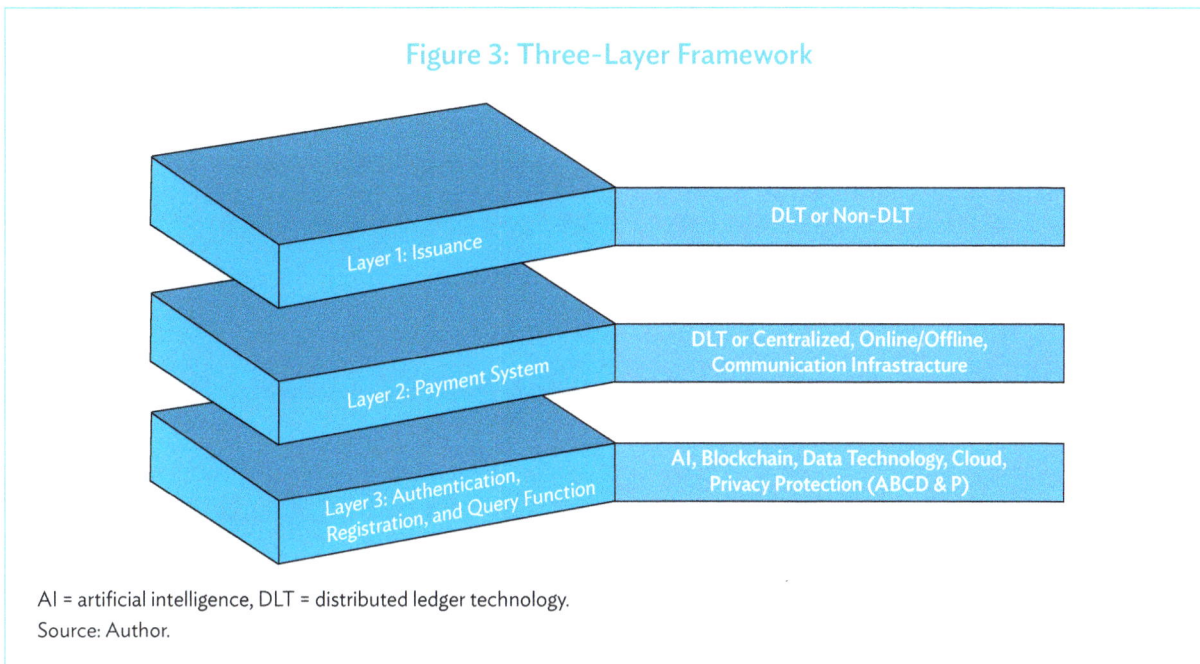

Figure 3: Three-Layer Framework

Layer 1: Issuance — DLT or Non-DLT

Layer 2: Payment System — DLT or Centralized, Online/Offline, Communication Infrastructure

Layer 3: Authentication, Registration, and Query Function — AI, Blockchain, Data Technology, Cloud, Privacy Protection (ABCD & P)

AI = artificial intelligence, DLT = distributed ledger technology.
Source: Author.

In the first layer, decisions have to be made on how a CBDC is being issued. For example, the central bank can choose between a centralized or distributed technology to sign and issue the encrypted digital string of money guaranteed by the central bank. Only the central bank can issue and burn (or remove from circulation) the digital money or tokens created. The first layer concerns the issuance, and the second layer is for payments. These two layers are concerned with how the digital currency is issued and what payment system is being used. Decisions may involve whether the currency is fully backed or just fractional-reserve based (for issuance), and cloud or DLT based (for the payment system).

The third layer consists of three clients: tokenization, registration, and analytics.[49] Tokenization or certification ensures supply is limited and determines whether the underlying is an asset or just created as a balance sheet item.

---

49   Tokens here refer to crypto tokens, which are digital representations of assets, currencies, physical objects, or services that reside on their own blockchains and represent an asset or utility.

There are also decisions about what biometric or recognition technology to use for KYC; what storage systems are capable of handling the data; what cloud or edge computing is needed; and the choice of data-analytic methods and digital devices, security, and privacy protection.[50] Tables 4 and 5 present the design and technology considerations for a CBDC.

Table 4: Central Bank Digital Currency Design

Design Considerations	Details
Ledger infrastructure	(i) Structure: distributed, centralized, decentralized, semi-decentralized, or hybrid. (ii) Payment verification: account-based or identity-based, token-based, value-based, hybrid. (iii) Digital identity verification: online checking, in-person checking, other proxies such as mobile numbers, biometric identity, self-sovereign identity.[a] (iv) Access: the access rights and data. (v) Functionality: simple transactions or to embed more complicated features, smart contracts or not, and protocols and cryptography (for CBDC with DLTs). (vi) Role and responsibilities: The responsibility of the public and private sector and the users. (vii) Governance: (a) What and who is being governed? (b) What and who is doing the governing? For example, governance of blockchains by humans, governance of humans by blockchains, governance of blockchains by blockchains, governance of humans by other humans.
Wallets and funds	(i) Digital wallet: types of hard or soft wallets and available applications, as well as design choices for user authentication, transaction authentication, and user interface incorporated within digital wallets. (ii) Funds in the wallet: interest or non-interest bearing (cash-like or deposit-like) and cap or limit on individual holdings. (iii) Scalability of large transaction volumes: possible ways include using multiple ledgers, off-ledger, or P2P transactions. (iv) Security of funds and transactions: KYC, anti-money laundering, counter-terrorist financing, limits, the means of access and control. (v) Technical and legal confidentiality protections: identity privacy, and transaction privacy (data privacy and program privacy).
Incentive	(i) Who bears the costs. (ii) Incentive for the merchants and individuals to use a CBDC. (iii) Directly covering costs from the public users or private service providers' business models.
Offline governance	This involves: (i) Changes to existing legislation and regulation, the extent to which CBDC is a public good. (ii) The process of identifying the priorities that include pain points and bottlenecks that hinder the mission of central banks. (iii) The setting of interest rates or to be interest-free. (iv) The need for and capabilities of monitoring online and offline transactions. (v) The party or parties responsible for KYC, AML, and counter-terrorist financing. (vi) Data policy including privacy protection and AI usage. (vii) The risk to the banking industry and individual banks. (viii) The implication of CBDC on other ministries, especially on fiscal policy. (ix) The flexibility of having an entirely new approach to policy, especially with blurring of the separation between monetary and fiscal policy.

AI = artificial intelligence, AML=anti money laundering, CBDC = central bank digital currency, DLT = distributed ledger technology, KYC = know your customer, P2P = peer to peer.

[a] Self-sovereign identity is an approach to digital identity that allows technology users to be in control of their identities. It is trustless in the sense that self-sovereign identity does not need a third party in establishing trust in an interaction. See Ferdous, Chowdhury, and Alassafi (2019).

Source: Bank for International Settlements, Brookings Institution, and author.

---

[50] State-of-art privacy protection methods such as secure multiparty computing, zero-knowledge proof, secret sharing, ring signature, and trusted execution environment are helpful. But these discussions are beyond the scope of this research.

Table 5: Central Bank Digital Currency Technology

Technology Considerations	Details
Convenient	Convenience can often bring a better user experience for consumers and improve the competitiveness of a central bank digital currency (CBDC). It requires that the design of a CBDC be used with or without bank accounts or smartphones. Smartphones, hardware wallet, stored value cards, and installed near-field communication devices are examples of good designs that will facilitate fast payment. Other special payment functions and gadgets (such as hard wallets, cards, and wearable terminals) are designed for users of special needs, such as children, the visually impaired, and the elderly. It is essential to apply offline payment function that can also be used in the environment of communication interruption and power failure.
Secure and resilient	Security and resilience are crucial to maintaining operational integrity. Security is one of the most important factors determining whether a CBDC will function well and be widely accepted. The system should be able to resist hacker attacks and be anti-counterfeiting. Many consider distributed ledger technologies or other cryptographic methods because they can reduce the risk of a single point of failure and make the CBDC system resistant to collapse, hacker attack, physical damage, and disasters. It can also support decentralized digital management to prevent large-scale data leakage. Security in design is needed for all use cases of CBDCs from the beginning. Operational security is ensured through continuous testing, verification of safeguards, adherence to best practices, and periodic external audits of major system components.
	The CBDC system should be operational across the country, 24 hours a day, 365 days a year, and highly resilient to operational failures and interruptions, disasters, power outages, and other issues. If the network connection is not available, the end user should have some ability to make offline payments. Local value storage solutions provide great resilience in such cases.
Fast and scalable	The process of money transfer or payment from the sender to receiver (individual or merchants) shall be completed as soon as possible or near real time and ensured. Technical scalability demands that the technologies supporting CBDC payment should be able to handle the ultra-high transaction capacity. Considering the potential large amount of transactions per second, the system needs to be both fast and scalable to ensure smooth transactions, settlement finality, and satisfying user experiences.
Interoperable	Interoperability is the key to the CBDC system, which will allow multiple CBDC systems to interact and exchange data with each other. This is especially important in the context of regional transactions. This ensures that any CBDC account can pay each other, and not limited by the provider payment interface, the CBDC system needs to provide full interaction with private sector digital payment systems and share the same infrastructure, code language, and standards-related regulatory systems.
Flexible and adaptable	Flexibility and adaptability are necessary for the CBDC system to satisfy the varying requirements. The existing financial system will be maintained for a long time. CBDCs can make payments more accessible, faster, and more effective, and the adaptability will enable it to be better incorporated into the existing financial system without jeopardizing stability. In the future, the demand for cross-border payment can also be met through the mutual adaptation of CBDC systems in various countries.
	Factors that determine the CBDC system's adaptability include the accuracy of the basic concepts of money and payment; the clarity of the related hierarchical design and the foresight of how the environment may evolve.

Source: Bank for International Settlements, author.

There is always a trade-off in adopting different designs, and not all pain points can be addressed thoroughly. The central pain point for cash or M0 is the high costs associated with the issuance, print, withdrawal, and storage of physical money as notes and coins. Physical cash lacks portability, traceability, and transparency. It is vulnerable to counterfeit mechanisms, money laundering, terrorism, and unknown criminal use. Meanwhile, existing noncash payment tools such as credit and debit cards, internet, and app payment cannot replace M0, as these are dependent on trusted third-party payment services. Further, these other payments depend on institutions' accounts that fail to support offline and anonymous payment services.

The CBDC proposition is the possibility of offline payment, managed anonymity, and P2P payment without a centralized ledger. The design can be viewed as M0.5 as it retains the P2P offline anonymity characteristics of M0, yet traceability is similar to M1. Unlike cards and institutional dependent payments, M0.5 can replace M0 with the added advantage of managed anonymity (Lee and Teo 2020). Nevertheless, some central banks are beginning to note the advantages of this new form of digital currency—which could transcend both traditional account-based money and physical cash (Carstens 2021).

This design showcases the best features of a distributed system, such as blockchain, with the central bank's central management. However, technical scalability issues typically associated with a decentralized ledger and the centralization levels or central management in a distributed ledger remain challenging. It is also important to understand the concept of online and offline governance.[51] In particular, what and who is being governed and what or who is doing the governing.

Technology and Opportunities

Technology and transaction costs

Technology and demand for money drive the evolution of fiat currency. The legal tender form has gradually transitioned from a physical to a digital-plus mobile form. The primary functions of money are a measure of value, a store of value, and a medium of exchange. Measurability, confirmability, and transferability are essential factors for realizing currency functions. Throughout history, productivity has spawned new demands, and technological innovation has pushed the evolution of money from physical, metal, and paper money to electronic and digital forms to improve currency circulation efficiency[52] and consumer welfare.

The P2P communication and DLT technological developments have triggered the review of the deposit currency system of commercial banks. Private and legal tender have coexisted throughout history. However, no matter how active these private currencies are, the country issues legal tender centrally because private currency issuance increases social transaction costs, which is the sum of private and external costs. The external costs result from private enterprises' rent-seeking behavior, especially if there is a monopolistic market structure. Governments treat legal tender as public infrastructure and ensure free and efficient service.

---

[51] According to McKie (2018), blockchains and governance can refer to at least four things: (i) governance of blockchains by humans (e.g., Ethereum Improvement Proposal, Bitcoin Improvement Proposal, and forks); (ii) governance of humans by blockchains (e.g., via Decentralized Autonomous Organizations or bounties); (iii) governance of blockchains by blockchains (e.g., on-chain limitations and permissions); and (iv) governance of humans (blockchain users/developers) by other humans (government authorities).

[52] For example, debit and credit card payments facilitate a more efficient system for monitoring and circulation. Debit and credit cards, while facilitating cash withdrawals from ATMs or retail outlets, also improve payment efficiency. However, it may also cause overborrowing if there are no safeguards for users, as well as a higher cost of transactions if both merchants and users have to pay higher costs.

To some, especially those in the developed markets, replacing the existing system of M1 and M2 causes a considerable waste of resources. For others, especially the developing markets, improving payment and remittances efficiency for financial inclusion, privacy protection, and managed anonymity are the ultimate objectives. Asia learned from crises and offline governance[53] that regulation and collaboration are still needed.

Dependence on cash in underserved areas is still too high and susceptible to money laundering, terrorism, and criminality. Public digital infrastructure is a supply-side issue for which governments are fully responsible, and if it is a public good, it must be freely available. Besides performing currency issuance and managing supply, central banks ensure a payment system that is assessable to all with a sound monetary policy for financial stability. Those seem to be the twin objectives of most central banks as discussions on CBDCs take shape with more precise definitions and taxonomy.

Other nascent technologies

The possible emergence of stablecoins like Diem has prompted G7 finance ministers and central bank governors to state that global digital currencies must meet all legal and regulatory requirements before being adopted. According to the US Office of the Controller of the Currency, federally chartered banks and thrifts may seek approval to participate in blockchain-based networks and use stablecoins for payment activities (Office of the Controller of the Currency 2021). With the legal status of stablecoins, these coins can access other countries and become a super-non-sovereign currency. This new non-sovereign has the potential to transform the existing monetary system, especially for smaller economies. The thinking and fear are that even if Diem or its equivalent does not become a primary digital currency, it can still function as a secondary global currency given its vast user base.

Regulators are researching the risk of digital currencies to financial stability and their complexity. While it is unhealthy for policy to front-run innovation, it is equally risky to have policy-lagging innovation. Policy makers are tooling up with knowledge and finding possible responses to new threats and risks of other e-money designs. Participation and collaboration with private institutions to design e-wallets and hardware are steps taken by central banks toward understanding the inner workings of these nascent CBDC and cryptocurrency technologies.

The other nascent technology is decentralized finance that pairs non-sovereign or sovereign money with tradeable tokens of goods and services. Tokens are the primary trusted carrier of value with technologies such as the Internet of Things. There are government initiatives to tokenize goods and promote e-wallets, gradually entering into insurance, financing, investment, trading, savings, logistic, supply chain, supply chain financing, and the entire economy. Governments such as in the PRC and Singapore see the potential of new business models, new products, and new customers via the token or digital asset economy. New laws and regulations are emerging for virtual assets and virtual asset service providers. The recent rise of fungible and non-fungible tokens with speculation calls for more regulatory oversight.[54]

---

[53]   Online governance is usually dictated by computer codes, while offline governance is more about decisions made by humans about what should be included in the computer codes and associated online processes.

[54]   A non-fungible token is a unit of data stored on a distributed ledger, usually a blockchain, that certifies a digital asset to be unique and therefore not interchangeable as in the case of fungible tokens. Non-fungible tokens can be used to represent items such as digital art, photos, videos, audio, and other types of digital files.

Implications for Financial Stability in Asia's Developing Economies

After the Asian financial crisis, government and central banks in Asia spent considerable time strengthening defenses against another similar crisis. Our discussion of CBDCs will be incomplete without referring to the Asian financial crisis and the implications of CBDCs for developing economies in Asia and the Pacific.

Risks for Asian developing economies

The high velocity and transmission speed are risk considerations for economies in the region given past experiences of sudden capital inflow and reversals during the Asian financial crisis. While there are many considerations, Hong Kong, China's linked exchange rate system seems to be working well for central banks with enough reserves. However, every economy is at a different stage of financial development and may not possess enough reserves and fiscal credibility to withstand major capital flights. Nevertheless, East Asian economies remained watchful of their competitiveness and flexibility with their link to the US dollar to improve competitiveness. In Project Bakong, a surge in Cambodia's blockchain payment system users might help address dollarization in the country (Nikkei Asia 2021) besides acquiring the ability to monitor the velocity and transmission speed. One objective of Project Bakong is to encourage the local currency and wean off US dollar dependency. While the digital local currency riel may be a good way to de-dollarize, there is a risk that the digital riel may not be able to maintain stability in the event of lack of liquidity or foreign reserves, or when the market has lost confidence in the financial position of the central bank.

The Project Bakong has both riel and US dollar as its central-bank-authorized reserves. The substitution effect between the two central-bank-authorized digital currencies will be an area for further study, especially the impact on the exchange rate. Rana (1998) summarized the choice of the exchange rate regime's considerations for Asia. The ability to curb excessive foreign capital inflows makes macroeconomic policies more independent. With central-bank-authorized digital currencies, exchange rates are an essential consideration for CBDC design.[55] It does not preclude central-bank-authorized digital currencies backed by other currencies, a basket of currencies, or a regional currency used by a trade bloc. The Project Bakong is a start to further development, such as cross-border payments and remittances between Cambodia and Malaysia. Cross-border public–private partnerships between the central bank and Maybank in Malaysia may enhance payment efficiency. This cross-border service is expected to benefit Cambodians residing in Malaysia and Malaysians in Cambodia, as well as businesses in both countries through the Bakong e-wallet and Maybank2u in cross-border fund transfer for trade settlement and remittances. But the higher velocity and transmission speed of CBDCs and payment systems may warrant more research to assess risk.

---

[55]   In many small and open economies, it is difficult to conduct monetary policy via interest rate policy, as a higher interest rate than global interest rates will attract inflow of capital. Monetary authorities in "open" economies may conduct exchange rate policy or interest rate policy but not both unless there is a restriction on capital flow. A higher interest rate will cause an inflow of capital and thus an appreciation of the currency. Similarly, a lower interest rate will lead to capital outflow and thus a lower exchange rate. Most open economy central banks conduct exchange rate policy to maintain a stable exchange rate and price stability. When there is excessive inflow of capital, the central bank will purchase debt instruments to increase the local money supply. Similarly, when there is an outflow of capital, central bank instruments are sold to decrease the local money supply. Such sterilization policy is highly dependent on the amount of central bank reserves and international confidence in the financial system.

Uncertainties facing Asian developing economies

(i)   Dependency on foreign currencies

Depending on the cross-border arrangement between the economies, CBDCs from larger economies might play a role in crowding out digital money from smaller economies. In particular, CBDCs backed by a single currency may lead to over dependence, losing the economic dependency in both fiscal and monetary policies. Dollarization and "yuanization" may both lead to unhealthy dependency of smaller economies relying on a major international fiat currency. In particular, monetary and fiscal policies may become less effective as the local currency is used less than foreign currency or other corporate or sovereign stablecoins, rendering the local currency irrelevant. One example is a popular and liquid stablecoin not approved by the foreign and local governments being used as the medium of exchange and a store of value in the digital economy, affecting the efficacy of monetary and fiscal policies. Gaming activities online among members of an international community may use a foreign sovereign or corporate stablecoin to transact and bypass the use of local fiat currency, digital or electronic. Without settlement through the formal financial system, it may be difficult to monitor, and tax revenue will be threatened.

(ii)   Financial imbalances

Allen (2000) argues that central banks and governments must avoid a rapid expansion of credit. Introducing new technology leads to uncertainty about future credit levels and financial crises, and is an essential consideration for the introduction of CBDCs. Higher asset prices will lead to higher credit levels and, in turn, higher asset prices. There is a need for appropriate regulation to minimize credit expansion's feedback effect by asset bubbles and the feedback loop's uncertainty between the two. Therefore, in introducing a CBDC, there is a need to monitor that new payments technology and new money will not lead to unintended credit expansion. Tokenizations that lead to complex fintech products may lead to a crypto-asset bubble. A transition to CBDC needs efforts to minimize credit expansion's uncertainty that may lead to a financial crisis. With traceability comes transparency, and the design of the CBDC matters. Given quantitative easing and massive asset purchases by central banks, transparency and information timing are more important to reduce uncertainty. A design that minimizes such information uncertainties can retain confidence and trust.

Williamson (2000) suggests using capital control even if both current and capital accounts' convertibility is desirable. Unfortunately, strengthening bank supervision, better bank management, and bank recapitalization has not led to more financial inclusion in lending to small and medium-sized enterprises and the underserved. Building up supervisory and managerial capacity to serve the underserved is less a concern to regulated institutions because of the higher compliance costs. CBDC technology may be a partial solution to better balance risk management and social objectives. With international digital remittances via e-wallets, a circuit breaker at the global level and a ceiling at the P2P level to stop rapid and massive capital outflows at crucial moments are technically feasible. With both timely information and real-time monitoring, uncertainties and rapid outflows are easier to address and manage with CBDCs, from a central bank perspective. In ASEAN, enormous effort and a cautious approach to new technology have led to a period of stability over the past 20 years, besides more flexible exchange rates, inflation targeting, and foreign reserve build-ups.

Digital reform and deep institutional changes are made possible by new technology, but they have to be accomplished and undertaken with a timeline that gives comfort, and after the issues and designs have been carefully considered and tested.

(iii)   Competition between CBDCs and deposits or sovereign bonds

With stablecoins and programmable CBDCs that can expire, there may be a substitution effect between CBDCs and deposits, and also local sovereign bonds. With CBDCs, there is also the uncertainty of borrowing in foreign CBDCs. While CBDCs may not be part of a country's settlement or clearing system, it will affect the exchange rates. But this may be beyond the control of the central bank, and close monitoring of CBDCs and new payment systems is needed. Digital tracking of transmission speed, velocity, and excessive credit expansion are all issues to be discussed.

In summary, the avoidance of contagion comes through regional effort and commitment. Such commitment comes only from a consensus and buy-in from all economies. Park et al. (2017) identify trigger factors for the Asian financial crisis as fixed exchange rates, currency mismatches, maturity mismatches, and inefficient allocation of foreign capital flows. Global responses to the Asian financial crisis included bilateral assistance, multilateral assistance, and regional cooperation initiatives. The most notable initiative was the Chiang Mai Initiative Multilateralization that addressed the balance of payments and short-term liquidity difficulties in ASEAN+3 members with a $240 billion financial arrangement.[56] The other impactful initiative was the Asian Bond Markets Initiative that addressed maturity mismatches. The initiative sought to develop efficient and liquid local currency bond markets to channel better Asia's vast savings to more productive long-term investments. The emphasis is on the timing and sequencing of financial liberalization, maintaining strong macroeconomic fundamentals, and improving financial efficiency and resilience through broad-based reforms. Balance sheet restructuring; more stringent prudential regulation and supervision; and meeting international best practices, core principles, and standards via institutional and legal frameworks are essential for long-term financial stability. Revisiting these issues and incorporating them when designing the CBDC leads to the principle of gradual implementation. A CBDC needs to demonstrate that its introduction leads to more transparency with e-wallet/e-accounts, better control of capital flows with circuit breakers, that it enhances capital formation via tokenized bonds, reduces contagion with regional collaboration/interoperability, and improves liquidity with pooling of stable or wrapped currencies (such as a regional CBDC).

Financial sector development issues, financial inclusion, domestic resource mobilization, capital revenue and taxes, a common ASEAN currency,[57] regional cooperation and coordination, financial stability, the digital divide, and domestic bond market development concerning CBDC development are areas that warrant further research and discussions.

---

[56]   ASEAN+3 includes the 10 member states of ASEAN, plus the PRC, Japan, and the Republic of Korea. There is an ASEAN+3 Macroeconomic Research Office, which is a regional macroeconomic surveillance organization that aims to help secure the macroeconomic and financial stability in the ASEAN+3 region.

[57]   While governments are focusing on the digital currency and electronic payments, talk of ASEAN currency has resurfaced because of the Triffin dilemma, i.e., the difficulties faced by reserve currency issuers trying to balance domestic monetary policy with other countries' demand for its reserve currency. However, the view is that "in the long run there will be a move towards monetary integration, but it doesn't work yet." While the short-term focus for some countries is promoting domestic use, a few Asian countries are already exploring different ways to achieve cross-border transactions of digital currency among national central banks. Scholars are now discussing the advantages of an ASEAN currency. "An Asian digital currency would help Asia to keep control of its own currency and financial destiny, rather than it being subject to the influence of the US dollar or the upcoming international digital currency—Libra or now known as the Diem dollar" (Pei 2021).

6   Conclusion

Digital currency in whatever form is the potential primary tool for the transition to a digital economy. To withstand the challenge from alternative currencies such as Diem and other stablecoins, governments in Asia have stepped up their efforts in developing digital infrastructure, digital currency supervision, digital asset market supervision, CBDC issuance, and related financial architecture. Cambodia, the PRC, Singapore, and Thailand have taken the lead.

Issues including needs, goals, digital financial infrastructure, and others, should be identified and discussed before authorities considering adoption of a CBDC. While many factors will influence how, when, and what will be adopted, strong public-private sector collaboration may determine its success. Before adoption, it is vital to examine interoperability. Strong national policy in the three countries examined closely in this paper has already brought about CBDC experiments and implementation. However, these nascent technologies may need to interact through intermediaries and across borders for mass adoption. These programs and initiatives are similar to bilateral or multilateral trade agreements in different phases and programs with the alignment of interests. Interoperability is crucial for economies with cross-border trade.

The potential next focus areas will most likely examine the scope of new multilateral platforms, global stablecoin arrangements, and CBDCs to address the challenges that cross-border payments face, without compromising minimum supervisory and regulatory standards to control risks to monetary and financial stability.

These initiatives may benefit global financial inclusion and sustainability as they bridge the gaps between the various CBDC initiatives and existing payment systems and other digital currencies to ensure success worldwide. Analysts believe that borderless, global commerce will be powered with the help of an interoperable protocol, as our global economic system is too multifaceted to be replaced by a singular currency (Guo Sky 2021).

Some may impact different areas or utility, and continuous research is vital in optimizing any CBDC and digital infrastructure design to take advantage of new developments in technology. Continuously improving CBDCs, exploring future paths, and revising implementation plans are becoming important central bank roles.

Finally, digital finance is going to be the future and its "impact surface" will be extensive. Countries are now prepared to participate in international regulatory coordination, promote regulatory consensus, and establish unified regulation standards. Unavoidably, the only and best way to achieve this is to be conversant in the technology, learn from the implementation, continuously review the existing regulation, and improvise whenever international dynamics change the landscape.

The benefits for CBDC cannot be fully realized unless there are (i) "greater and higher quality connectivity between economies" through distributed computing and public digital infrastructure; (ii) "expanded global and regional trade and investment opportunities" via digital access to capital and free trade; and (iii) increased and diversified regional public goods such as distributed ledger and blockchain for trade traceability, identity, supply chain financing, and tokenization of products and services. The disclaimer is that CBDC will also bring with it new risks and challenges. The benefits of adoption must outweigh the costs. The difficulties remain when these nascent technologies surprise us with unanticipated dangers and complexities.

The Asian Development Bank's Operational Priority 7 states that regional cooperation and integration operations are expected to enhance connectivity and competitiveness, promote regional public goods, strengthen cooperation in the finance sector, and strengthen subregional initiatives. CBDCs, designed with Priority 7 in mind, may provide more transparency, narrow the digital divide, lower the financial and remittance charges, and increase trade and other financing access. CBDC projects may deepen the capital market with transparent, low-cost, liquid tokenized bond markets with payment versus payment, and delivery versus payment. Inclusive fintech is now widely available. Technology is less an issue, but education, collaboration, digital infrastructure building, capacity, resources, and financing remain pain points. Issues of capacity building are important and may need addressing before the introduction of a CBDC. In particular, communication infrastructure and fintech literacy may help advance sustainable economic growth via the digital economy that has a well-designed CBDC. Also, the digital economy consumes a large amount of energy and therefore contributes to carbon emissions. Green tech and green financing are therefore issues to be discussed and cannot be separated from the CBDC, which is essentially digital. Given that the risk and complexities of CBDCs are still relatively unknown, it is, therefore, no surprise that the investigations and research will go on for some time.

APPENDIX 1
Road Map Summary of the G20, Asia, and New Zealand Central Bank Digital Currency Projects

Table A1.1: Central Bank Digital Currency Roadmap and Projects for G20

Country	Latest Project	Other Project
United States	United States central bank digital currency (CBDC) (research, wholesale): On May 2022, the United States Federal Reserve published a paper to discuss whether and how a CBDC could improve the safe and efficient domestic payments system and seek for comments. https://www.federalreserve.gov/publications/money-and-payments-discussion-paper.htm	Project Hamilton (research, retail) https://www.bostonfed.org/publications/one-time-pubs/project-hamilton-phase-1-executive-summary.aspx
Canada	Canada CBDC (research, wholesale): The Bank of Canada says it is building the capability to issue CBDCs so it can be ready should the need arise. Currently, Canada does not have plans to issue a digital currency. https://www.bankofcanada.ca/research/digital-currencies-and-fintech/projects/central-bank-digital-currency/	Jasper (pilot, wholesale) https://www.bankofcanada.ca/wp-content/uploads/2017/05/fsr-june-2017-chapman.pdf
Saudi Arabia	Aber (pilot, wholesale) According to Project Aber report (2020): A joint digital currency and distributed ledger Project launched by Saudi Central Bank and Central Bank of the United Arab Emirates. The project achieved its key objectives, including using a new distributed ledger technology based solution for real time cross-border interbank payments between commercial banks without the need to maintain and reconcile Nostro accounts with each other. https://www.sama.gov.sa/en-US/News/Documents/Project_Aber_report-EN.pdf	
Australia	Australia retail CBDC (research, retail): The Reserve Bank is collaborating with the Digital Finance Cooperative Research Centre to explore use cases for CBDC in Australia. The Australian Treasury is participating as a member of the steering committee. https://www.rba.gov.au/media-releases/2022/mr-22-23.html	Project Atom (2020, proof of concept, wholesale) https://www.rba.gov.au/media-releases/2021/mr-21-30.html

continued on next page

Table A1.1 continued

Country	Latest Project	Other Project
India	India CBDC (Proof of concept, retail, wholesale): The Reserve Bank of India released a concept note to explain the objectives, choices, benefits, and risks of issuing a CBDC in India. The Reserve Bank will soon commence pilot launches for specific use cases. https://rbi.org.in/scripts/BS_PressReleaseDisplay.aspx?prid=54510	
Russian Federation	Digital Ruble (announced in 2020, pilot): In 2022, the Bank of Russia and market participants launched the testing of the digital ruble platform and completed the first digital ruble transfers between individuals. https://cbdctracker.org/currency/russian_federation-digital_ruble	
South Africa	South Africa CBDC (research, retail): According to the South African Reserve Bank, it has investigated the feasibility, desirability, and appropriateness of CBDC as electronic legal tender, for general-purpose retail use, complementary to cash. https://www.resbank.co.za/en/home/publications/publication-detail-pages/media-releases/2021/SARB-commences-feasibility-study-for-a-general-purpose-retail-central-bank-digital-currency	Khokha (research, wholesale) https://www.resbank.co.za/content/dam/sarb/publications/media-releases/2022/project-khokha-2/Project%20Khokha%202%20Summary%20Report%206%20April%202022.pdf
Türkiye	Digital lira (proof of concept, retail): According to the Central Bank of the Republic of Türkiye (CBRT), for the first phase of the pilot study, the central bank will develop a prototype "Digital Turkish Lira Network" and run limited closed-circuit pilot tests with technology stakeholders. Based on the results of those tests, the CBRT will unveil advanced phases of the pilot study that will reflect broader participation. The CBRT also plans to carry out tests that may diversify the coverage of the Digital Turkish Lira research and development (R&D) project into areas such as blockchain technology, use of distributed ledgers in payment systems, and integration with instant payment systems. The results of the first phase will be announced in 2022 after the tests are completed. https://www.tcmb.gov.tr/wps/wcm/connect/42756019-bc96-4828-822d-b52ce396eded/ANO2021-40.pdf?MOD=AJPERES&CACHEID=ROOTWORKSPACE-42756019-bc96-4828-822d-b52ce396eded-nLF93ki	
Argentina	Argentina CBDC (research, retail) https://www.bcra.gob.ar/PublicacionesEstadisticas/Resumen.asp?id=1579	

continued on next page

Table A1.1 continued

Country	Latest Project	Other Project
Brazil	Digital Real(proof of concept, retail): According to local media outlet Estadao, the president of the Central Bank of Brazil said plan to start a pilot program of a digital currency in 2022. https://www.bcb.gov.br/detalhenoticia/17632/nota	
Mexico	Mexico CBDC (research, retail): According to Ledger insight, governor of the Bank of Mexico, Victoria Rodríguez Ceja, confirmed plans to release a retail CBDC during 2025. https://www.ledgerinsights.com/mexico-plans-a-retail-cbdc-by-2025/	
France	France CBDC (pilot, wholesale): According to the Banque de France, in partnership with the European Investment Bank and Société Générale - FORGE, the Banque de France successfully carried out on 28 April an experiment on the use of CBDC for settling digital bonds issued by the European Investment Bank on a blockchain. https://www.banque-france.fr/en/communique-de-presse/experiment-use-central-bank-digital-currency-cbdc	France CBDC (pilot, wholesale) https://www.banque-france.fr/en/communique-de-presse/banque-de-france-press-release-20-july-2020
Germany	According to Deutsche Bundesbank, Deutsche Börse, Deutsche Bundesbank, and Germany's Finance Agency have developed and successfully tested a settlement interface for electronic securities. In doing so, the participants have demonstrated that it is possible to establish a technological bridge between blockchain technology and conventional payment systems to settle securities in central bank money with no need to create central bank digital currency. https://www.bundesbank.de/en/press/press-releases/dlt-based-securities-settlement-in-central-bank-money-successfully-tested-861444	
Italy	The Bank of Italy publishes an article to introduce CBDC https://www.bancaditalia.it/media/notizia/a-digital-euro-a-contribution-to-the-discussion-on-technical-design-choices/	Italian Banking Association launches digital euro research project in 2020 and does not mention any involvement from the country's central bank https://www.ledgerinsights.com/italian-banking-association-launches-digital-euro-project/
United Kingdom	United Kingdom CBDC (research, wholesale and retail): According to Bank of England, it published a discussion paper in March 2020. In April 2021, the Bank of England and HM Treasury announced the joint creation of a CBDC taskforce. https://cbdctracker.org/currency/united_kingdom-rscoin	United Kingdom CBDC (research, wholesale) https://www.mas.gov.sg/-/media/MAS/ProjectUbin/Cross-Border-Interbank-Payments-and-Settlements.pdf?la=en&hash=5472F1876CFA9439591F06CE3C7E522F01F47EB6

continued on next page

Table A1.1 continued

Country	Latest Project	Other Project
China, People's Republic of	e-CNY (pilot, retail): According to the People's Bank of China (PBOC), it has initiated pilot programs in some representative regions. The PBOC will continue to prudently advance the pilot e-CNY R&D project in line with the People's Republic of China's 14th Five-Year Plan, with no preset timetable for the final launch. http://www.pbc.gov.cn/en/3688110/3688172/4157443/4293696/2021071614584691871.pdf	
Indonesia	Digital rupiah (research, retail): According to Bank Indonesia, it continues to research CBDC and plans to issue a white paper on the development of Digital Rupiah. https://www.bi.go.id/en/publikasi/ruang-media/news-release/Pages/sp_2417722.aspx	
Japan	Japan CBDC (proof of concept, retail): The Bank of Japan completes the proof of concept Phase 1 to investigate the basic functions that are core to CBDC in March 2022 as scheduled. In April 2022, the central bank moves on to phase 2, in which it implements various additional functions of CBDC in the test environment developed in Phase 1 and investigates feasibility and challenges. https://www.boj.or.jp/en/announcements/release_2022/rel220325f.pdf	Stella (research) https://www.boj.or.jp/en/announcements/release_2020/rel200212a.htm/
Korea, Republic of	Republic of Korea CBDC (proof of concept, retail): According to Coingeek, the country is to start real-world testing of a CBDC with 10 commercial banks. The phase was expected to conclude before 2022 ends, as the Bank of Korea says it plans to publish an updated report on the CBDC project by the end of the year. This report will be its final one before it decides on whether or not to release a CBDC. There has been no update since June 2022 according to CBDC Tracker. https://coingeek.com/south-korea-to-start-real-world-testing-of-cbdc-with-10-commercial-banks-report/	https://cbdctracker.org/currency/south_korea

e-CNY = electronic Chinese yuan, G20 = Group of Twenty.
Source: Author

Table A1.2: Central Bank Digital Currency Roadmap for Other Asian Countries and New Zealand

Country	Latest Project
New Zealand	New Zealand CBDC (proof of concept, retail): The Reserve Bank of New Zealand is commencing CBDC proof-of-concept design work. https://www.rbnz.govt.nz/hub/news/2022/02/innovation-key-to-the-future-of-money-and-cash
Brunei Darussalam	According to Ledger insights, Brunei Darussalam has not publicly mentioned a CBDC project. https://www.ledgerinsights.com/indonesia-finalizing-wholesale-cbdc-design-joining-other-asean-states/
Cambodia	Bakong (launched,retail): Bakong, developed by Japanese blockchain company Soramitsu, enables Cambodians to use a free mobile app to make payments and transfer money through bank on the platform, even if they do not have a traditional account with the bank. https://www.reuters.com/markets/rates-bonds/cambodia-aims-hybrid-digital-currency-blockchain-unbanked-2021-12-22/
Lao People's Democratic Republic (Lao PDR)	Laos CBDC (research, retail). According to ledger insights, the Bank of the Lao PDR is partnering with Japanese blockchain provider Soramitsu to explore the potential of a CBDC. https://www.bol.gov.la/en/index
Malaysia	Malaysia CBDC: (i) 2021–2022, explores cross-border wholesale CBDC via Project Dunbar; (ii) 2022–2023, explores domestic wholesale CBDC; (iii) Beyond 2023, explores domestic retail CBDC. https://www.bnm.gov.my/documents/20124/5915429/fsb3_en_box3.pdf
Philippines	Philippines CBDC (proof of concept, wholesale): The Bangko Sentral ng Pilipinas initiated an exploratory study in 2021. A national payment system assessment identified relevant use cases of a wholesale CBDC aimed at enhancing the payment system's safety, resiliency, and efficiency. It then targets rollout in the near term of pilot CBDC implementation (Project CBDCPh). The project aims to build organizational capacity and hands-on knowledge of key aspects of CBDCs relevant for a use case addressing frictions in the national payment system. https://www.bsp.gov.ph/SitePages/MediaAndResearch/SpeechesDisp.aspx?ItemId=915
Singapore	Project Orchid (in preparation but no intention to launch, retail); Project Ubin (proof of concept, wholesale); Project Dunbar (cross-border experiment). https://www.mas.gov.sg/news/parliamentary-replies/2022/reply-to-cos-cut-on-digital-sing-dollar https://www.mas.gov.sg/schemes-and-initiatives/Project-Ubin https://www.mas.gov.sg/publications/monographs-or-information-paper/2022/project-dunbar https://www.mas.gov.sg/news/media-releases/2022/mas-partners-the-industry-to-pilot-use-cases-in-digital-assets
Thailand	Project Inthanon-LionRock (proof of concept, wholesale): The scope of Project Inthanon,originally focused on interbank payments, expanded to support innovation in business sectors. Its prototype shows that the supply chain financing industry can be transformed by smart contract features on blockchain. https://www.bot.or.th/English/FinancialMarkets/ProjectInthanon/Documents/20210308_CBDC.pdf
Viet Nam	Viet Nam CBDC (research, retail) https://vanbanphapluat.co/decision-942-qd-ttg-2021-development-of-e-government-with-orientations-towards-2030

CBDC = central bank digital currency.
Source: Author

APPENDIX 2
Payments and Settlement Systems in Asia

Country	System	Established	Operator
Brunei Darussalam	1. Real-Time Gross Settlement System (RTGS)	2014	Authoriti Monetari Brunei Darussalam
	2. Automated Clearing House Cheque Clearing	2016	The Brunei Association of Banks
	3. Automated Clearing House Direct Credit	2017	
Cambodia	1. National Clearing System	2012	National Bank of Cambodia
	2. FAST System	2016	
	3. Cambodia Shared Switch	2017	
	4. Bakong Blockchain Payment System	2020	
Indonesia	1. BI Real-Time Gross Settlement - Gen I/Gen II	2000/2015	Bank Indonesia (BI)
	2. BI Scripless Securities Settlement System - Gen I/Gen II	2004/2015	
	3. Sistem Kliring Nasional Bank Indonesia Gen1/ Gen II National Clearing System For Debit and Credit Clearings	2005/2015	
	4. BI Electronic Trading Platform	2018	
Lao PDR	1. Gross Settlement System (RTS/X)/RTGS	2011/2019	Bank of the Lao PDR (the central bank of the Lao PDR)
	2. Lao Payment and Settlement System (LaPASS) For Wholesale	2020	
	3. Lao National Payment Network (LAPNET) For Retail	2020	
Malaysia	1. Real-Time Gross Settlement system - RENTAS system	1999	Bank Negara Malaysia. The Malaysian Electronic Payment System (MEPS) is an interbank network service provider in Malaysia set up in 1997. In August 2017, MEPS merged with Malaysian Electronic Clearing Corporation Sdn Bhd (MyClear) to form Payments Network Malaysia Sdn Bhd (PayNet). HOUSe, started operation in 2006, is owned by four locally incorporated foreign banks.
	2. National Electronic Cheque Information Clearing System - eSPICK	2009	
	3. Interbank GIRO	2010	
	4. Financial Process Exchange	2004	
	5. Direct Debit (PayNet)	2010	
	6. MEPS and HOUSe Shared ATM Network	2006	
Philippines	1. Real-Time Gross Settlement System - PhilPaSS	2002	Bangko Sentral ng Pilipinas
	2. National Retail Payment System - InstaPay and PESONet (The Philippine EFT System and Operations Network) Automatic Clearing Houses	2017	

Country	System	Established	Operator
Singapore	1. New MAS Electronic Payment System (MEPS+)	1998	Monetary Authority of Singapore
	2. Continuous Linked Settlement	2003	...
	3. Clearing and Payment Services Pte Ltd (CAPS)	2001	DBS/UOB/OCBC
	4. Singapore Dollar Cheque Clearing System	2019	Banking Computer Services Pte Ltd
	5. US Dollar Cheque Clearing System	1996	Banking Computer Services Pte Ltd
	6. Cheque Truncation System	2003	Singapore Automated Clearing House
	7. Interbank GIRO	2001	Singapore Automated Clearing House
	8. ATM networks	...	...
	9. MEPS+-SGS (Singapore Government Securities)	1998	Monetary Authority of Singapore
Thailand	1. BAHTNET System	1995	Bank of Thailand
	2. Imaged Cheque Clearing System and Archive System	...	Bank of Thailand
Viet Nam	1. Electronic/Paper Clearance & Interbank Electronic Payment Systems	2007	State Bank of Vietnam
	2. Bank Card Switching and Clearing System	...	State Bank of Vietnam
	3. Securities Clearing and Settlement System	...	State Bank of Vietnam
	4. Internal and Bilateral Payment Systems	...	Credit Institutions
China, People's Rep. of	1. China National Advanced Payment Systems – High Value Payment System	2005	People's Bank of China
	2. China National Advanced Payment Systems – Bulk Entry Payment System	2006	CCDC
	3. China Domestic Foreign Currency Payment System	2008	
	4. The Cheque Imaging System	2007	
	5. The Internet Banking Payment System	2010	
	6. Local Clearing Systems	...	
	7. SHCH Clearing System	...	
	8. SD&C Securities Settlement System	...	
	9. CCDC Central Bond Generalized System	1981	
Japan	1. BOJ-NET Funds Transfer System	1988	Bank of Japan
	2. Zengin System	1973	Japanese Banks Payment Clearing Network (ZenginNet)
	3. Foreign Exchange Yen Clearing System	1980	
	4. Bill and Cheque Clearing Systems	1980	Japanese Bankers Association
Korea, Republic of	1. BOK-Wire+	2009	Bank of Korea
	2. Retail Payment System	1994	KFTC
	3. Securities Settlement System	1988	Korea Securities Depository, Korea Exchange
	4. Foreign Exchange Settlement System	1996	CLS Bank

Country	System	Established	Operator
References	Japan		https://www.boj.or.jp/en/paym/outline/pay_boj/pss1212a.pdf
	Korea, Republic of		https://www.bok.or.kr/eng/main/contents.do?menuNo=400045
	China, People's Republic of		https://wiki.treasurers.org/wiki/China#Clearing_and_payment_systems
			https://www.bis.org/cpmi/publ/d105_cn.pdf
	Brunei Darussalam		https://bab.org.bn/corporate-information/cheque-clearing-fund-transfer/
	Cambodia		https://www.nbc.org.kh/english/payment_systems/background_of_payment_systems.php
	Lao People's Democratic Republic		https://www.cma.se/customers/national-banks/central-bank-laos.html
	Indonesia		https://www.readkong.com/page/payment-clearing-and-settlement-systems-in-indonesia-8299877
	Malaysia		http://docshare04.docshare.tips/files/25092/250929060.pdf
	Philippines		https://www.bsp.gov.ph/Pages/PAYMENTS%20AND%20SETTLEMENTS_deletethis/National%20Retail%20Payment%20System/National-Retail-Payment-System.aspx
	Singapore		https://www.bis.org/cpmi/publ/d97_sg.pdf
	Thailand		https://www.bot.or.th/English/PaymentSystems/Publication/PS_Annually_Report/Documents/Payment_2019_E.pdf
	Viet Nam		https://www.sbv.gov.vn/webcenter/portal/en/home/sbv/paytreasury/paysystem?_afrLoop=5967029792966506#%40%3F_afrLoop%3D5967029792966506%

... = not available, CCDC = China Central Depository & Clearing, KFTC = Korea Financial Telecommunications & Clearings Institute, Lao PDR = Lao People's Democratic Republic, SHCH = Shanghai Clearing House, UOB = United Overseas Bank.

Source: Author.

Central Bank Digital Currency Literature Review

Cross-Border Payments and Regional Flows

1. Bank for International Settlements (BIS), International Monetary Fund (IMF), and World Bank. 2021. *Central Bank Digital Currencies for Cross-Border Payments: Report to the G20*. https://www.bis.org/publ/othp38.pdf.

The retail (money transfer operation) and wholesale (banking network) sides of cross-border payments are plagued with inefficiencies brought about by high fees and lack of interoperability of payment systems due to differences in domestic legislation. On the wholesale side, these include differences in the implementation of anti-money laundering/combatting the financing of terrorism standards, rules on settlement finality, participation criteria for payment systems with central bank money settlement, rules on the conflict of laws, and others.

Central bank digital currencies (CBDCs) present opportunities for central banks to simplify and enhance the performance of cross-border payments, increase transaction speed through 24/7 availability, and decrease costs. According to a survey of central banks in 2020, cross-border payment efficiency (especially wholesale) is an important motivation in CBDC development.

The BIS, the IMF, and the World Bank (2021) illustrate that cross-border payments through CBDCs can be envisioned in two fundamentally different ways: (i) a retail CBDC of a given jurisdiction becomes available to anybody inside and outside of that jurisdiction, with no specific coordination between the issuing central banks; and (ii) access and settlement arrangements are established among different retail and/or wholesale CBDCs, built on strong cooperation among central banks.

In the first scenario of international use, the CBDC could be designed so that it faces no constraints on where and by whom it is used. If the design allows for anonymous payments like cash, it would by default be accessible to foreign residents. Similar systems are being developed (e.g., People's Republic of China electronic Chinese yuan [e-CNY] and the Eastern Caribbean Currency Union [DCash]) and launched in the Bahamas (Sand Dollar).

The second scenario constitutes a coordinated design framework including technological, market structure, and legal aspects, aiming to facilitate cross-border interoperability of multiple CBDCs from different jurisdictions. Auer, Haene, and Holden (2021) present this in more detail.

2. R. Auer, P. Haene, and H. Holden. 2021. Multi-CBDC Arrangements and the Future of Cross-Border Payments. *BIS Papers*. No. 115. Basel. https://www.bis.org/publ/bppdf/bispap115.pdf.

Auer, Haene, and Holden (2021) highlight the inefficiencies of the existing correspondent bank arrangements for cross-border payments: (i) operation costs to sustain cross-border banking relations and prefunding, (ii) mismatch of opening times across time zones, (iii) mismatch of communication standards, (iv) unclear foreign exchange rates and unclear income fees, (v) limited transparency on the status of payment, and (vi) high costs of compliance across borders. Among these, the mismatch of standards and compliance (e.g., legal and regulatory) across borders is the greatest source of friction.

While central banks across the world have initiated efforts to increase interoperability between existing payment systems, many central banks are also exploring the benefits of CBDCs on cross-border payments. Auer, Haene, and Holden (2021) explore three multi-CBDC (mCBDC) models that tackle the three dimensions of payment system interoperability: (i) compatible CBDC systems, (ii) interlinked CBDC systems, and (iii) a single system for mCBDC. Early cooperation in the development of CBDCs can help avoid the rigors of *post hoc* coordination exercises.

- Model 1: Compatible CBDC takes advantage of the clean slate of nascent CBDC systems. It encourages central banks to cooperate in the design of CBDC in a uniform international standard.
- Model 2: Interlinked CBDC systems promote a shared technical interface, supported by contractual agreements between the systems that allow participants in one to make payments to those in another
- Model 3: A single system for mCBDC encourages central banks to agree on a single rulebook, a single set of participation requirements, and supporting infrastructure.

Contagion Risk

3. BIS, IMF, and World Bank. 2021. *Central Bank Digital Currencies for Cross-Border Payments: Report to the G20.* Basel: BIS. https://www.bis.org/publ/othp38.pdf.

The ease of cross-border payments from CBDCs can increase contagion effects, and sudden capital flow reversals that can undermine economic and financial stability. Market integration offers investment and risk-sharing opportunities, and hedging that increase contagion risk. With higher gross capital flows and potentially less-effective capital flow management measures if they can be circumvented (due to nascent stage of development), countries may find it harder to manage their financial conditions and exchange rates, or freely choose their exchange rate regime. Global financial conditions could be transmitted more readily around the world, complicating policy tradeoffs. Hence, today's large share of countries managing their exchange rates could be pushed toward more open capital accounts and flexible exchange rates, thus needing to maintain an effective and independent monetary policy. While CBDCs are still in their nascent stage and the pattern of net capital flows is more difficult to predict, many mCBDC pilots have already been initiated and illustrated how these frameworks could help in removing frictions in cross-border payments. For example:

- Project Jasper-Ubin: A 2016 Bank of Canada and Monetary Authority of Singapore (MAS) project that explores the use of distributed ledger technology (DLT) for clearing and settling of payments and securities. The project has effectively demonstrated cross-platform interoperability given the realistic assumption that DLT-based real-time gross settlement (RTGS) systems in each country sit on different platforms—in this case, the Jasper network (in Canada) sat on Corda and the Ubin network (in Singapore) sat on Quorum. In 2020, the project was expanded with the development of a production-grade blockchain-based multi-currency settlement network, which enabled issuance or distribution of digital currencies (both wholesale CBDC and commercial bank money) in various currencies, and which included interfaces for other blockchain networks to connect and integrate seamlessly.
- Project Jura: Conducted by the Bank of France, the Swiss National Bank, and the BIS Innovation Hub, together with a private sector consortium, explores cross-border settlement with two wholesale CBDCs and digital security on a DLT platform.

- Project Inthanon-LionRock: A project between the Bank of Thailand and the Hong Kong Monetary Authority. In the Project Inthanon-LionRock operating model, cross-border payments are processed through a "corridor network" which links up two separate domestic wholesale CBDC networks and provides cross-border settlement services.

- Project mCBDC Bridge: The project is run by the BIS Innovation Hub in collaboration with the Hong Kong Monetary Authority, Bank of Thailand, Digital Currency Institute of the People's Bank of China, and the Central Bank of the United Arab Emirates. The mCBDC Bridge is a multi-currency CBDC platform that adopts DLT to facilitate real-time cross-border funds transfers and pursues the path of atomic payment-versus-payment for foreign exchange transactions.

- Project Dunbar: Project initiated by BIS Innovation Hub Singapore Centre and MAS. The project explores enhancements to a multi-CBDC platform through: (i) the use of smart contracts to automate foreign exchange based on the discovery of and matching with the best available rates, and to manage liquidity and foreign exchange risks, and (ii) exploring how different multi-currency settlement platforms could be designed to link up with one another.

- Project Aber: Project between the Saudi Central Bank and the Central Bank of the United Arab Emirates. The model adopted a new CBDC issued by both central banks as a unit of settlement between commercial banks in the two countries and domestically. The Aber model is based on a permissioned DLT that enables a high level of decentralization and enables commercial banks to settle with each other even in cases where the central bank is unavailable or disconnected from the network.

Exchange Rate

4. BIS. 2018b. *Central Bank Digital Currencies*. Basel: BIS. https://www.bis.org/cpmi/publ/d174.pdf

The way in which access to CBDCs is granted implies that substitution effects will affect different types of financial assets. CBDCs that pay interest and are readily transferable would likely be attractive to professional financial market participants and may substitute for money market instruments such as foreign exchange swaps. Policy makers should introduce different forms of quantitative limits or caps on the use or holdings of CBDCs as a way of controlling potentially undesirable implications or to steer usage in a certain direction. For example, facilitating one-to-one convertibility of CBDCs with reserves and bank notes is required to prevent breaking the unit of currency and maintain exchange rate parity between different types of central bank money.

5. M. Ferrari, A. Mehl, and L. Stracca. 2020. Central Bank Digital Currency in an Open Economy. *European Central Bank Working Paper Series.* No 2488. Frankfurt. https://www.ecb.europa.eu/pub/pdf/scpwps/ecb.wp2488~fede33ca65.en.pdf.

Ferrari, Mehl, and Stracca (2020) illustrate that a CBDC with fixed (positive) remuneration and limited restrictions on foreign transactions would increase the international spillovers of a monetary policy shock, thereby increasing international linkages. Without limits, a CBDC creates a new arbitrage condition that links the interest rate differential, the exchange rate, and the remuneration of the CBDC. Specifically, that arbitrage condition defines the risk-free rate in the foreign economy as a mark-up on the remuneration of the CBDC. This leads to stronger exchange rate movements in response to shocks in the presence of a CBDC—foreign agents rebalance much more into a CBDC than they would into bonds, if the latter were the only internationally traded asset, because of the CBDC's hybrid nature. However, the magnitude of these shocks can be dampened through tight restrictions such as limits on foreigner transactions and adjustment of CBDC rates flexibly.

6. BIS. 2021a. CBDCs: An Opportunity for the Monetary System. In *BIS Annual Economic Report 2021*. pp. 65–95. Basel: BIS. https://www.bis.org/publ/arpdf/ar2021e3.htm.

One major concern against the use of CBDCs in cross-border payment is exacerbating the risk of currency substitution (digital dollarization) whereby a foreign digital currency displaces the domestic currency to the detriment of financial stability and monetary sovereignty. However, the risks of currency substitution from cross-border use of CBDCs may be limited and could be addressed largely through international monetary cooperation. A foreign currency is unlikely to gain a domestic foothold just because of its digital nature, the widespread use of a currency—and, in extremes, dollarization—is hinged on factors such as the depth, efficiency, and openness of a country's financial markets, trust in a currency's long-run value, and confidence in the institutional and legal infrastructure.

Still, there are safeguards against substitution risk as central banks can restrict non-residents' access to their currency to certain permitted transactions only. These kinds of policies might reduce the risk of volatile flows and currency substitution in recipient economies. Such restrictions would resemble existing rules governing how non-residents can open a bank account outside their home country.

Financial Stability

7. European Central Bank (ECB). 2021. Report on a Digital Euro. Frankfurt.

This report examines the issuance of a CBDC—the digital euro—from the perspective of the Eurosystem. Looking at the banking sector, the introduction of a digital euro could affect the transmission of monetary policy and have a negative impact on financial stability. High demand for a digital euro might induce depositors to transform their commercial bank deposits and increase their funding costs. The ECB notes that a non-interest-bearing or positive interest-bearing digital euro is more likely to induce large-scale substitution away from deposits in a negative interest rate environment.

As a result, banks might have to replace deposits with central bank borrowings attached to safe assets collateral (e.g., public sector securities, financial entity debt, etc.), or expensive market-based capital funding. Higher funding costs can lead to a decrease in banks' ability for financial intermediation leading to less supply of credit, the greater cost for borrowers and lost economic activity. Additionally, the loss of a bank's deposit-taking function will lead to further information asymmetry that would harm its risk assessment capacity. In turn, the change in the banking sector's traditional business can drive banks to riskier assets with negative effects on financial stability.

8. M. Mancini-Griffoli, M. Peria, I. Agur, A. Ari, J. Kiff, A. Popescu, and C. Rochon. 2018. Casting Light on Central Bank Digital Currency. *IMF Staff Discussion Note*. Washington, DC.

Similar to ECB (2021), Mancini-Griffoli et al. (2018) include a discussion on the impact on bank deposits of CBDCs with characteristics of bank deposits (traceability and protection from loss or theft). It assesses two hypothetical scenarios: (i) risk of disintermediation in tranquil times and (ii) run risk in times of systemic financial stress. During the first scenario, banks can try to offset loss deposits through higher funding costs. This includes increasing deposit rates and subsequently lending rates (at the cost of lower loan demand), and shifting to market-based funding. Higher funding costs will lead to lower profitability and the possibility of a shift to higher-risk investments and assets that will have a negative impact on financial stability. Additionally, loss of deposits will lead to disintermediation of the banking sector. While central banks could limit the decline in bank deposits and lending by setting limits on individual CBDC holdings; discouraging, (such as through fees) convertibility from bank deposits to CBDC, or lending directly to banks, the central bank's balance sheet would grow, taking on more credit risk. The second scenario discusses the impact of CBDC during financial stress. It concludes that CBDC is unlikely to matter during a general crisis as there are much safer and more liquid alternatives.

9. T. Richards, C. Thompson, and C. Dark. 2020. Retail Central Bank Digital Currency: Design Considerations, Rationales and Implications. *Reserve Bank of Australia Bulletin*. September. https://www.rba.gov.au/ publications/bulletin/2020/sep/retail-central-bank-digital-currency-design-considerations-rationales-and-implications.html.

The introduction and wide adoption of a CBDC can represent a significant change in the structure of a financial system—particularly in the demand for bank deposits. While some of the demand for a CBDC might come from switching out of cash, there might also be switching out of bank deposits. Currently, commercial banks source about 60% of their funding from deposits, with about two-thirds of that being at-call deposits. If banks were to experience an outflow of deposits, they would have to fund more of their lending in capital markets or from equity. The loss of deposit funding and greater reliance on other funding sources could result in some increase in banks' cost of funds and result in a reduction in the size of their balance sheets and in the amount of financial intermediation. Of course, this would depend on any changes to the structure of the central bank's assets resulting from the increase in its balance sheet, for example, whether it invested in government securities as opposed to lending funds back to banks or buying their securities.

Source: Asian Development Bank.

APPENDIX 4
Basic Functions of Money

Revisiting the basic function of money will help us understand the pain points of payment systems. Table A4 describes the different types of digital money and their pain points.

Table A4: Technological Bottlenecks and Pain Points of Digital Money

e-Money Functions	Explanation	Central Bank Digital Currency Non-DLT Based	Non-Central Bank Digital Currency DLT Based
Medium of exchange	E-money functions as a reference value to facilitate trade.	Digitizing coins and notes to have minimal impact on the fractional reserve system.	Limited supply, low acceptance, low circulation, low transaction per second, high energy consumption for some coins, congestion, high storage cost, high transaction fees, no finality, governance issues.
Store of value	E-money is an asset that can be saved, retrieved, and exchanged at a later time, and be predictably useful when retrieved, and it also maintains value without depreciating.	No different from the existing system.	Illiquidity, universally recognizable, readily exchangeable for other assets, fluctuates in value.
Unit of account	E-money allows different things to be compared to each other.	May be able to digitize other goods and services not traded frequently.	Not a standard measure for trade in goods and services, not a benchmark to measure the value.
Standard of deferred payments	E-money is a widely accepted way to value debt, thereby allowing goods and services to be acquired now and paid for in the future.	New products on digitized goods and services.	Inflation and deflation, no recourse in case of counterfeit, instability and loss of purchasing power.
Attributes	Requirements	Advantages	Disadvantages
Portability	Money is mobile and can be exchanged with ease with other currencies.	More portable than cash and notes with possible 24/7 exchange.	In reference to fiat currencies, there needs to be a regulated exchange.
Durability	Money is immutable and can withstand continuous use by a large number.	Forgery is more complicated and there is no wear and tear.	May lose its value if there is a loss of trust with attacks or bugs.
Divisibility	Money has small increments for the exchange of things of varying value.	E-money can have more than two decimals.	Divisible up to 10–8.

continued on next page

Table A4 continued

e-Money Functions	Explanation	Central Bank Digital Currency Non-DLT Based	Non-Central Bank Digital Currency DLT Based
Verifiability	Money is impossible to forge and easily identifiable as legitimate.	E-money is comparatively more traceable, authenticated, and verified.	Double spend and subject to malicious attack if there are faults or bugs.
Fungibility	Money is interchangeable in that two equal units have to be equivalent and indistinguishable.	Fractional e-money can have many digits and is an advantage of its fungibility.	It is possible to trace the transaction history and the individuals who use them.
Limits in supply	Money can retain its value.	If backed and conditional on fiat, it is relatively stable.	It can be created with no limits.

DLT = distributed ledger technology.
Source: Author.

Global Central Bank Digital Currency Developments

Table A5.1 summarizes central bank digital currency (CBDC) designs and corresponding use cases worldwide.

Table A5.1: Recent Use Cases by Central Banks

Target	Technology	Country/region	Considerations
General public or retail	Central bank digital currencies (CBDCs) without distributed ledger technology (DLT)	Uruguay A consumer-oriented system without the need for internet connection. Commercial banks did not participate in the pilot system.	(i) How to measure the impact of CBDCs on the banking system? Will this increase the financing cost of banks? (ii) Will this be conducive to the transmission of monetary policy?
General public or retail	CBDC with DLT	Canada, People's Republic of China (PRC), India, Israel, Lithuania, Marshall Islands, Sweden, Senegal, Thailand, Tunisia DLT here refers to using some or all of the features of cryptocurrency. In the case of the PRC, unspent transaction output[a] or unspent transaction output from bitcoin transactions are used to balance the ledger. DLT may allow the emerging economy to leapfrog as it solves many pain points for developing economies such as payment, trading, and financing.	(i) Can developing economies enhance financial inclusion? (ii) Can developing economies bypass the traditional International Payment or remittance system to lower overall cost? (iii) Can household activities and illiquid be tokenized and be integrated with CBDC in the form of utility and asset tokens?
Financial institutions or wholesale	CBDC for wholesale	Euro area, Canada, Singapore, Thailand, South Africa, Japan This is the most popular proposal that can integrate the traditional payment system and banking models.	(i) Are there benefits beyond efficiency improvement using reserve deposits, crypto tokens or assets? (ii) How does the payment system integrate with other financial instruments and processes such as delivery and payment for securities, supply chain financing, and cross-country remittances?

[a] In cryptocurrencies, an unspent transaction output is an abstraction of electronic money with a ledger that can only append entries. Each unspent transaction output represents a chain of ownership implemented as a chain of digital signatures where the owner signs a message transferring ownership of their unspent transaction output to the receiver's public key. Public key infrastructure is a set of requirements that allow the creation of digital signatures, among other things. Through it, each digital signature transaction includes a private key and a public key. Digital signature is used in Bitcoin to as proof one owns the private key without having to reveal it (so proves that one is authorized to spend the associated funds).

Sources: S. Shiral. 2019. Central Bank Digital Currency: Concepts and Trends. VOX CEPR Policy Portal. https://voxeu.org/article/central-bank-digital-currency-concepts-and-trends; M. L. Bech, and R. Garratt. 2017. Central Bank Cryptocurrencies. *BIS Quarterly Review*. September. https://www.bis.org/publ/qtrpdf/r_qt1709f.htm; and author.

Table A5.2 looks at the classification of projects and the interoperability of each.

Table A5.2: Notable Retail Central Bank Digital Currency Projects

Country/ Region	CBDC Type and Architecture Models[a]	Architecture (direct/indirect claim)	Infrastructure (conventional or DLT)	Access (account or token based)	Interoperability (National or international digital currency) (able to perform cross-border payments)
Bahamas	Retail–2 tier Issuance	Direct (Hybrid)	DLT	Account-Based (would require national digital ID)	National
Cambodia	Retail–2 tier Issuance	Direct (Hybrid) tiered know-your-customer system where end users can open a low-transfer-limit account using SMS verification	DLT (Hyperledger Iroha)	Both (account and token-based to cater to tiered KYC system where end users can open a low-transfer-limit account using SMS verification)	National
PRC	Retail–2 tier Issuance	Direct (Hybrid) Payment Claim counterparty risks transferred to Banks	Hybrid (central database and DLT payment network)	Token-based at tier 2 (electronic payment)	National (There is brief literature on working with bilateral experiments with Singapore's Project Ubin)[b] to test international interoperability
Sweden e-Krona (2020)	Retail–2 tier issuance	Direct claim (Hybrid)	DLT based	Both (account and token-based) (Token claim: issued and redeemed only by the central bank)[c]	National (Part of G7 CBDC collaboration testing led by Bank for International Settlements)[d]
Eastern Caribbean Central Bank (DXCD)	Retail–2 tier issuance	Direct claim (Hybrid)	DLT based	Token Claim	International (It focuses on four pilot countries, i.e., Antigua and Barbuda, Grenada, Saint Christopher (St Kitts) and Nevis and Saint Lucia. DXCD is a digital version of the Eastern Caribbean Currency.
Ukraine	Retail–2 tier Issuance	Direct	Hybrid	Undefined	National

continued on next page

Table A5.2 continued

Country/ Region	CBDC Type and Architecture Models[a]	Architecture (direct/indirect claim)	Infrastructure (conventional or DLT)	Access (account or token based)	Interoperability (National or international digital currency) (able to perform cross-border payments)
Uruguay	Retail	Direct (Did not include any banks during pilot)	Hybrid used centralized digital wallets that operated through state-owned telecommunications provider Antel,[c] but used cryptographic ePesos	Token Claim (Anonymity of peer-to-peer transaction)	National

CBDC = central bank digital currency, DLT = distributed ledger technology, G7 = group of 7, ID = identification, KYC = know your customer, PRC = People's Republic of China, SMS = short messaging service.

[a] Direct CBDC: Retail services with direct claim on central bank; Hybrid CBDC: two tiers with the intermediatory handling retail payments; Intermediated CBDC: two-tiered wholesale ledger only; Indirect or synthetic CBDC: Indirect claim on central bank (general purpose CBDC) intermediary bank to fully back liabilities to client with claims on central bank.

[b] Ledger Insights. 2020. Singapore MAS Exec Says All That's Missing for a CBDC Is a Central Bank Decision. 22 July. https://www.ledgerinsights.com/mas-says-cbdc-just-needs-central-bank-decision/.

[c] KPMG. 2020. Whitepaper: A Global Look at Central Bank Digital Currencies: From Iteration to Implementation. https://www.tbstat.com/wp/uploads/2020/08/The-Block-Research-CBDC-Report-From-Iteration-to-Implementation_v1.04.pdf.

[d] Ledger Insights. 2020. Seven Central Banks, BIS Publish Digital Currency Report that Considers Sharing Payment. 9 October. data https://www.ledgerinsights.com/central-bank-digital-currency-cbdc-sharing-payment-data/.

Source: Author.

Below are three of many examples of wholesale CBDC research studies conducted through the collaborative efforts of central banks.

Table A5.3: Wholesale Central Bank Digital Currency Focused Collaborations

Economy	Asset Transfer Method	Technology Used across Experiment Stages	Interoperability Strategy
Thailand— Hong Kong, China (Project Inthanon-LionRock)	Tokenized wrapped central bank digital currency (W-CBDC) is wrapped by a central-bank-issued depository receipt to facilitate foreign exchange settlement.	Both economies signed a memorandum of understanding to explore cross-border payments. The focus is on delivery versus payment, and payment versus payment in a distributed ledger technology (DLT) environment via various models of cross-border payments using a network called "Corridor Network."	DLT-based "Corridor Network" was designed for settlement on Corda. Use of tokenized W-CBDC provided local currency liquidity on the enabled DLT *Corridor Network via* embedded foreign exchange transactions mechanism in various foreign exchange models in an atomic payment versus payment manner.[a] To put it in simple terms, atomic payment versus payment manner or swaps will enable people to directly trade with one another wallet-to-wallet.
Japan—European Central Bank (Project Stella)	Digital yen and digital base money	Phase 1: Used DLT to process large-scale payments. Phase 2: Tested Securities settlement in a DLT setting. Phase 3: Applied DLT-related technologies to improve cross-border payment efficiency. Phase 4: Focused on the confidentiality and auditability of settlement assets, such as CBDC, in a DLT environment.	"Cross-chain atomic swap" (which does not require ledgers to be interconnected when using digital signatures and hashed timelock contracts),[b] the atomic settlement was made possible for delivery versus payment on DLT. For cross-border payments: on-ledger escrow using hashed timelock contracts proved the possibility that synchronized settlement between different types of ledgers—ensuring the safety of cross-border payment using synchronized payment methods that secure funds along the payment chain, to achieve mitigating of credit risk exposure.
Singapore—Canada (Ubin –Jasper Project)	Tokenized Singapore dollar— Digital Canadian dollar (deposit receipts (fiat)-backed tokens)	In Phase 4 of Project Ubin and Phase 3 of Project Jasper: Testing cross-border payments with DLT systems under different models including W-CBDC, proved a prototype commercial blockchain network for multi-currency payments to improve cross-border payment functionality. Project Jasper used Corda and Project Ubin used Quorum.	Achieved cross-border (Canada and Singapore), cross-digital currency (Canadian and Singapore dollars), and cross-blockchain platform (Corda with Quorum) atomic transactions using hashed timelock contracts without needing a third party to facilitate the transaction.

CBDC = central bank digital currency.

[a] An automatic transfer of funds is a standing banking arrangement whereby transfers between a customer's two (or more) accounts are made on a regular, periodic basis under specified conditions. Automatic transfers are executed without further instruction or action by the customer; a common way that automatic transfers are executed is through "sweep" instructions, whereby all excess funds in one account are swept into another account. The automatic transfer of funds is one core offering of both commercial and online banks. With smart contracts and in the tokenized network, the transfer is autonomous from one e-wallet to another and executed completely. https://www.investopedia.com/terms/a/automatic-transfer-of-funds.asp.

[b] A hashed timelock contract is a type of smart contract used in blockchain applications to eliminate counterparty risk by enabling the implementation of time-bound transactions. In practical terms, this means that recipients of a transaction have to acknowledge payment by generating cryptographic proof within a certain timeframe. Otherwise, the transaction does not take place. https://www.investopedia.com/terms/h/hashed-timelock-contract.asp.

Source: Author.

All three notable wholesale CBDC projects in Table A5.3 have identified the use of hash-locking technology as the successful interoperability A3 strategy when testing cross-border transactions across two payment systems. The hashed timelock contract mechanism is only cross-dependent; whereby interoperation between different blockchains is triggered usually a hash of the random number to be discussed. It is a trust-based model that is immune to any 51% attack,[1] making it suitable for cross-chain exchanges. However, it is not suitable for cross-chain asset transfer. Therefore, a cross-border payment network has to be complemented by other interoperability mechanisms such as relay technology (as used in the Hong Kong, China–Thailand project via the corridor network), whereby the asset is wrapped to provide liquidity for the asset transfer to occur.

---

[1]   Ledgers are validated by a participating nodes or institutions in the network. If the nodes collude or control majority of the computing power, they can cast doubts on the integrity of the ledger. Once the trust of the ledger is lost, the assets or CBDCs that are tracked by the ledger will be compromised. A 51% attack refers to an attack on an open blockchain, or trustless ledger in which no one is trusted, by a group of miners or validators of the ledgers by controlling more than 50% of the network's computing power. There are, however, different consensus algorithms to validate the ledger without being subject to this type of attack. A trust-based ledger or private blockchain verifies the identity of the nodes with user agreement, and is less likely to be subject to 51% attacks with trusted nodes.

Bilateral and Multi-Central-Bank Digital Currency System

The Bank for International Settlements (BIS) is involved with several central banks in cross-border payments at the central bank digital currency (CBDC) design phase. If CBDCs interoperate with digital currencies from other economies, it may improve payment efficiency. The multi-CBDC (mCBDC) system is an active research area. There are four projects involving wholesale bilateral and mCBDCs.

These experiments demonstrate that cross-border CBDC activities involving CBDCs are operationally feasible and may improve efficiency. However, the experiments have raised questions about monetary policy, legal issues, and economic implications. While these projects were different in cases and designs, they generally involved the payments versus payments, or payments versus delivery of digitized or tokenized assets. All four projects are distributed ledger technology (DLT) based.

Project Inthanon-LionRock 2

Project Inthanon-LionRock2 (ILR2) is led by the BIS Innovation Hub (Hong Kong branch), together with the Hong Kong Monetary Authority (HKMA) and the Bank of Thailand (BIS 2021b). Building on the original Project Inthanon-LionRock project by the HKMA and Bank of Thailand, ILR2, the goal of the extended project was to explore the use of DLT for facilitating real-time cross-border funds transfers using an atomic-payment-versus-payment mechanism for foreign exchange transactions between the two jurisdictions (BIS 2021b).

Project Jura

This project is led by the BIS Innovation Hub (Switzerland branch), together with the Bank of France, the Swiss National Bank, and a private sector consortium, including the SIX Digital Exchange to explore the transfer between euro and Swiss franc wholesale CBDCs, between two commercial banks using DLT operated by a third party. Tokenized asset and foreign exchange trades were settled using payment-versus-payment and delivery-versus-payment mechanisms.[1]

Project Dunbar

Project Dunbar is led by the BIS Innovation Hub (Singapore branch), alongside the Reserve Bank of Australia, Bank Negara Malaysia, the Monetary Authority of Singapore, and the South African Reserve Bank. Technical prototypes are developed on two different DLT platforms—Corda and Quorum. The Corda platform development was led by R3, while the Quorum platform development was led by Partior (with support from DBS,

---

[1]   Banque de France. 2021. Cross-Border Settlement Using Wholesale CBDC. https://www.bis.org/publ/othp44.pdf.

J.P. Morgan, and Temasek). There are now two prototypes that facilitate—over a single platform—direct cross-border settlements between financial institutions using multiple fiat digital currencies.[2]

Project Inthanon-LionRock: M-CBDC Bridge

M-CBDC, or the M-CBDC Bridge project, is led by the Hong Kong, China branch. The initiative is an extension of the Project Inthanon-LionRock project between Thailand and Hong Kong, China. With the involvement of the BIS, the central banks of the People's Republic of China; Hong Kong, China (HKMA); Thailand; and the United Arab Emirates are developing a shared DLT system where they can use their own CBDCs for cross-border payments. Multiple central banks can issue their own CBDC and distribute it to participants on the DLT platform. These participants can in turn conduct peer-to-peer payments and redeem the CBDC for reserves at the issuing central bank.

According to a report, the 22 private participants include several banks from Hong Kong, China and the United Arab Emirates, and six international banks, apart from the People's Republic of China banks. The international banks are HSBC and Standard Chartered, which previously participated in the Thailand–Hong Kong, China cross-border CBDC trials, as well as Goldman Sachs, Société Générale, UBS, and Singapore's DBS.[3]

---

[2] FST Media. 2022. RBA joins successful prototype of CBDC settlements platform. https://fst.net.au/financial-services-news/rba-joins-successful-prototype-of-cbdc-settlements-platform/; BIS. 2022a. Project Dunbar: International Settlements Using Multi-CBDCs. https://www.bis.org/publ/othp47.pdf; MAS. 2022. BIS Innovation Hub and Central Banks of Australia, Malaysia, Singapore and South Africa Develop Experimental Multi-CBDC Platform for International Settlements. https://www.mas.gov.sg/news/media-releases/2022/experimental-multi-cbdc-platform-for-international-settlements.

[3] Ledger Insights. 2021. China's 6 State Owned Banks Part of M-CBDC Bridge SWIFT Replacement. 4 November. https://www.ledgerinsights.com/chinas-6-state-owned-banks-part-of-m-cbdc-bridge-swift-replacement/; BIS. 2022b. mBridge: Building a multi CBDC platform for international payments. https://www.bis.org/publ/brochure_mbridge.pdf

References

Adrian, T. and T. Mancini-Griffoli. 2019a. The Rise of Digital Currency. *VoxEU*. 9 September. https://voxeu.org/article/rise-digital-currency.

Adrian, T., and T. Mancini-Griffoli. 2019b. The Rise of Digital Money. Fintech Notes, Washington, DC. https://www.imf.org/~/media/Files/Publications/FTN063/2019/English/FTNEA2019001.ashx.

Allen, F. 2000. *Financial Structure and Financial Crisis*. Manila: Asian Development Bank. https://www.adb.org/sites/default/files/publication/157203/adbi-rp10.pdf.

Auer, R. and R. Böhme. 2020a. The Technology of Retail Central Bank Digital Currency. Paper. Bank for International Settlements (BIS), Basel. https://www.bis.org/publ/qtrpdf/r_qt2003j.pdf.

Auer, R. and R. Böhme. 2020b. CBDC Architectures, the Financial System, and the Central Bank of the Future. https://cepr.org/voxeu/columns/cbdc-architectures-financial-system-and-central-bank-future

Auer, R. G. Cornelli, and J. Frost. 2020. Rise of the Central Bank Digital Currencies: Drivers, Approaches and Technologies. *BIS Working Papers*. no. 880. Basel. https://www.bis.org/publ/work880.pdf.

Auer, R., P. Haene, and H. Holden. 2021. Multi-CBDC Arrangements and the Future of Cross-Border Payments. BIS Papers. No. 115. Basel. https://www.bis.org/publ/bppdf/bispap115.pdf.

Bank for International Settlements (BIS). 2016. A Glossary of Terms Used in Payments and Settlement Systems. Basel. https://www.bis.org/dcms/glossary/glossary.pdf?scope=CPMI&base=term.

Bank of Canada. 2018. Should the Central Bank Issue E-Money. Working paper. Ottawa. https://www.bankofcanada.ca/wp-content/uploads/2018/12/swp2018-58.pdf.

Bank of England. 2018. Central Bank Digital Currencies—Design Principles and Balance Sheet Implications. *Staff Working Paper*. No. 725. London. https://www.bankofengland.co.uk/-/media/boe/files/working-paper/2018/central-bank-digital-currencies-design-principles-and-balance-sheet-implications.

Bank of England. 2021. Bank of England Statement on Central Bank Digital Currency. https://www.bankofengland.co.uk/news/2021/april/bank-of-england-statement-on-central-bank-digital-currency.

Bank of Thailand. 2020. The Outcomes and Findings of Project Inthanon-LionRock and the Next Steps. https://www.bot.or.th/English/AboutBOT/Activities/Pages/Inthanon_LionRock.aspx.

Banque de France. 2021. Cross-Border Settlement Using Wholesale CBDC. https://www.bis.org/publ/othp44.pdf.

Bank of Thailand. 2021. The Way Forward for Retail Central Bank Digital Currency in Thailand. https://www.bot.or.th/Thai/DigitalCurrency/Documents/BOT_RetailCBDCPaper.pdf.

Bech, M. L., U. Faruqui, and T. Shirakami. 2020. Payments Without Borders. *BIS Quarterly Review*, March 2020. https://www.bis.org/publ/qtrpdf/r_qt2003h.htm.

Bech, M. L. and R. Garratt. 2017. Central Bank Cryptocurrencies. *BIS Quarterly Review.* September. https://www.bis.org/publ/qtrpdf/r_qt1709f.htm.

BIS. 2018a. E-Payments in Asia - Regulating Innovation and Innovative Regulation. Keynote address by Jacqueline Loh, Deputy Managing Director of the Monetary Authority of Singapore, at the Central Bank Payments Conference. Singapore. 26 June 2018. https://www.bis.org/review/r180727f.htm.

BIS. 2018b. *Central Bank Digital Currencies*. Basel: BIS. https://www.bis.org/cpmi/publ/d174.pdf.

BIS. 2000. Survey of Electronic Money Developments. *CPMI Papers* No. 38. Committee on Payments and Market Infrastructures. Basel. https://www.bis.org/cpmi/publ/d38.htm#:~:text=Electronic%20money%20products%20are%20defined,device%20in%20the%20consumer's%20possession.&text=A%20number%20of%20publications%20relating,the%20auspices%20of%20the%20BIS.

BIS. 2020a. *Central Bank Digital Currencies: Foundation Principles and Core Features*. Report no. 1 in a series of collaborations from a group of central banks. Basel: BIS. https://www.bis.org/publ/othp33.pdf.

BIS. 2020b. Innovations in Payments for Wholesale. https://www.bis.org/publ/qtrpdf/r_qt2003f.htm.

BIS. 2020c. The Technology of Retail Central Bank Digital Currency. *BIS Quarterly Review*. Basel. https://www.bis.org/publ/qtrpdf/r_qt2003j.htm.

BIS. 2021a. CBDCs: An Opportunity for the Monetary System. In *BIS Annual Economic Report 2021*. pp. 65–95. Basel: BIS. https://www.bis.org/publ/arpdf/ar2021e3.htm.

BIS. 2021b. Project Inthanon-LionRock to mBridge: Building a Multi CBDC Platform for International Payments. A joint report by the BIS Innovation Hub Hong Kong Centre, the Hong Kong Monetary Authority, the Bank of Thailand, the Digital Currency Institute of the People's Bank of China and the Central Bank of the United Arab Emirates. https://www.bis.org/publ/othp40.htm https://www.hkma.gov.hk/media/eng/doc/key-functions/financial-infrastructure/Inthanon-LionRock_to_mBridge_Building_a_multi_CBDC_platform_for_international_payments.pdf

BIS. 2022a. Project Dunbar: International Settlements Using Multi-CBDCs. https://www.bis.org/publ/othp47.pdf

BIS. 2022b. mBridge: Building a multi CBDC platform for international payments. https://www.bis.org/publ/brochure_mbridge.pdf

BIS, IMF, and World Bank. 2021. *Central Bank Digital Currencies for Cross-Border Payments: Report to the G20.* Basel: BIS. https://www.bis.org/publ/othp38.pdf.

Boar, B., H. Holden, and A. Wadsworth. 2020. Impending Arrival – A Sequel to the Survey on Central Bank Digital Currency. BIS Working paper. No. 107. https://www.bis.org/publ/bppdf/bispap107.htm.

Boar, B. and A. Wehrli. 2021. Ready, Steady, Go? – Results of the Third BIS Survey on Central Bank Digital Currency. *BIS Working Paper.* No. 114. https://www.bis.org/publ/bppdf/bispap114.htm.

Bossu, W., M. Itatani, C. Margulis, A. D. P. Rossi, H. Weenink, and A. Yoshinaga. 2020. Legal Aspects of Central Bank Digital Currency: Central Bank and Monetary Law Considerations. *IMF Working Papers.* Washington, DC. https://www.imf.org/en/Publications/WP/Issues/2020/11/20/Legal-Aspects-of-Central-Bank-Digital-Currency-Central-Bank-and-Monetary-Law-Considerations-49827.

Businesswire. 2021a. Global Mobile Wallet Market (2021 to 2026) - Growth, Trends, COVID-19 Impact, and Forecasts - ResearchAndMarkets.com. 14 June. https://www.businesswire.com/news/home/20210614005331/en/Global-Mobile-Wallet-Market-2021-to-2026---Growth-Trends-COVID-19-Impact-and-Forecasts---ResearchAndMarkets.com;

Businesswire. 2021b. Global Digital Remittance Market Analysis 2021–2028 by Type (Inward, Outward), & Channel (Banks, Money Transfer Platforms, Online Platforms) - ResearchAndMarkets.com. 28 September. https://www.businesswire.com/news/home/20210928005629/en/Global-Digital-Remittance-Market-Analysis-2021-2028-by-Type-Inward-Outward-Channel-Banks-Money-Transfer-Platforms-Online-Platforms---ResearchAndMarkets.com

Carstens, A. 2021. Digital Currencies and the Future of the Monetary System. Remarks by Agustín Carstens, General Manager, Bank for International Settlements at the Hoover Institution policy seminar. Basel. 27 January. https://www.bis.org/speeches/sp210127.pdf.

Clifford, J. 2019. Intro to Blockchain: UTXO vs Account Based. 20 September. https://medium.com/@jcliff/intro-to-blockchain-utxo-vs-account-based-89b9a01cd4f5.

Coindesk. 2021. Inside Bakong: How Cambodia Hopes to Leapfrog Into the Future with Digital Currency. 6 March. https://www.coindesk.com/tv/money-reimagined/money-reimagined-mar-6-2021-20210303.

CPMI. 2020. Enhancing Cross-Border Payments: Building Blocks of a Global Roadmap. Stage 2 report to G20. BIS, Basel.

Equalocean. 2020. China's National Digital Currency, DCEP, Is on the Way – But Will It Involve Blockchain? 15 February. https://equalocean.com/analysis/2020021513599.

European Central Bank (ECB). 2021. Report on a Digital Euro. Frankfurt. https://www.ecb.europa.eu/euro/html/digitaleuro-report.en.html.

European Parliament. 2019. *The Future of Money.* Brussels: European Union. https://www.europarl.europa.eu/cmsdata/190218/IPOL_STU(2019)642364_EN-original.pdf.

Falempin, L. 2020. What Does COVID-19 Mean for Central Bank Digital Currencies (CBDCs)? *Tokeny.* 14 May. https://tokeny.com/what-does-covid-19-mean-for-central-bank-digital-currencies/.

Federal Reserve. 2021. What is a Central Bank Digital Currency?

Ferdous, M. S., F. Chowdhury, and M. O. Alassafi. 2019. In Search of Self-Sovereign Identity Leveraging Blockchain Technology. *IEEE Access.* 7: 103059–103079. doi:10.1109/ACCESS.2019.2931173. ISSN 2169-3536.

Ferrari, M., A. Mehl, and L. Stracca. 2020. Central Bank Digital Currency in an Open Economy. *ECB Working Paper Series*. No 2488. https://www.ecb.europa.eu/pub/pdf/scpwps/ecb.wp2488~fede33ca65.en.pdf.

Financial Stability Board (FSB). 2020. *Enhancing Cross-border Payments: Stage 3 Roadmap.* Basel: FSB. https://www.fsb.org/2020/10/enhancing-cross-border-payments-stage-3-roadmap/.

Forkast. 2021. Cambodian State Digital Currency Sees Strong Uptake. 6 August. https://forkast.news/headlines/cambodias-cbdc-sees-strong-uptake/.

FST Media. 2022. RBA Joins Successful Prototype of CBDC Settlements Platform. 23 March. https://fst.net.au/financial-services-news/rba-joins-successful-prototype-of-cbdc-settlements-platform/.

Khmer Times. 2021. Cambodia Explores Cross-Border Transactions of CBDC-like Bakong, Now Used By 200,000 People. 9 August. https://www.khmertimeskh.com/50911542/cambodia-explores-cross-border-transactions-of-cbdc-like-bakong-now-used-by-20000-people/.

G20. 2021. Central Bank Digital Currencies for Cross-Border Payments. July 2021. Report to the G20. https://www.riksbank.se/globalassets/media/nyheter--pressmeddelanden/nyheter/2021/report-to-the-g20-central-bank-digital-currencies-for-cross-boarder-payments.pdf.

G20. 2022. Options for Access to and Interoperability of CBDCs for Cross-Border Payments. July 2022.

Guo Sky. 2021. Interoperability Will Determine CBDC Winners and Losers. *Cointelegraph.* 2 February. https://cointelegraph.com/news/interoperability-will-determine-cbdc-winners-and-losers.

Hong Kong Monetary Authority (HKMA). 2021a. eHKD: A Technical Perspective. https://www.hkma.gov.hk/media/chi/doc/key-functions/financial-infrastructure/e-HKD_A_technical_perspective.pdf.

HKMA. 2021b. Joint Statement on the Multiple Central Bank Digital Currency (m-CBDC) Bridge Project. Press release. 23 February. https://www.hkma.gov.hk/eng/news-and-media/press-releases/2021/02/20210223-3/.

International Monetary Fund (IMF). 2020a. *A Survey of Research on Retail Central Bank Digital Currency.* Washington, DC: IMF. https://www.imf.org/en/Publications/WP/Issues/2020/06/26/A-Survey-of-Research-on-Retail-Central-Bank-Digital-Currency-49517.

IMF. 2020b. Casting Light on Central Bank Digital Currencies. IMF Staff Discussion Note. Washington, DC. https://www.imf.org/en/Publications/Staff-Discussion-Notes/Issues/2018/11/13/Casting-Light-on-Central-Bank-Digital-Currencies-46233.

Kosse, A. and I. Matte. 2022. Gaining Momentum – Results of the 2021 BIS Survey on Central Bank Digital Currencies. *BIS Papers* No 125. Basel.

KPMG. 2020. Whitepaper: A Global Look at Central Bank Digital Currencies: From Iteration to Implementation. https://www.tbstat.com/wp/uploads/2020/08/The-Block-Research-CBDC-Report-From-Iteration-to-Implementation_v1.04.pdf.

Lai, R. 2016. Understanding Interbank Real-Time Retail Payment System. *Handbook of Blockchain Volume 1.* Amsterdam: Elsevier.

Lai, R. 2018. *Understanding Interbank Real-Time Retail Payment Systems. Handbook of Blockchain, Digital Finance and Inclusion.* Amsterdam: Elsevier.

Ledger Insights. 2020. China's Digital Currency to Start Pilots. 9 December. https://www.ledgerinsights.com/china-central-bank-digital-currency-pilot-cbdc-dcep/.

Ledger Insights. 2021. China's 6 State Owned Banks Part of M-CBDC Bridge SWIFT Replacement. 4 November. https://www.ledgerinsights.com/chinas-6-state-owned-banks-part-of-m-cbdc-bridge-swift-replacement/.

Lee, D. 2015. *Digital Currency: Handbook of Digital Currency: Bitcoin, Innovation, Financial Instruments, and Big Data.* Elsevier, Academic Press.

Lee, D and E. Teo. 2020. The New Money: The Utility of Cryptocurrencies and the Need for a New Monetary Policy. *Disintermediation Economics.* pp. 111–172.

Lee, D., L. Yan, and W. Yu. 2021. A Global Perspective on Central Bank Digital Currency. *China Economic Journal.* 14: pp. 52–66.

Mancini-Griffoli, M., M. Peria, I. Agur, A. Ari, J. Kiff, A. Popescu, and C. Rochon. 2018. Casting Light on Central Bank Digital Currency. *IMF Staff Discussion Note.* Washington, DC.

McKie, S. 2018. Blockchain Communities and Their Emergent Governance: Thoughts on Legitimacy and Narratives. *Amentum.* 19 November. https://medium.com/amentum/blockchain-communities-and-their-emergent-governance-cfe5627dcf52.

Monetary Authority of Singapore (MAS). 2017. Project Ubin Phase 2: Re-Imagining Interbank Real-Time Gross Settlement System Using Distributed Ledger Technology. https://www.mas.gov.sg/-/media/MAS/ProjectUbin/Project-Ubin-Phase-2-Reimagining-RTGS.pdf?la=en&hash=02722F923D88DE83C35AF4D1346FDC2D42298AE0.

MAS. 2021a. A Retail Central Bank Digital Currency: Economic Considerations in the Singapore Context. https://www.mas.gov.sg/publications/monographs-or-information-paper/2021/retail-cbdc-paper.

MAS. 2021b. Singapore and Thailand Launch World's First Linkage of Real-time Payment Systems. News release. 29 April. https://www.mas.gov.sg/news/media-releases/2021/singapore-and-thailand-launch-worlds-first-linkage-of-real-time-payment-systems.

MAS. 2021c. MAS Partners IMF, World Bank and Others to Launch Global Challenge for Retail CBDC Solutions. News release. 28 June. https://www.mas.gov.sg/news/media-releases/2021/mas-partners-imf-world-bank-and-others-to-launch-global-challenge-for-retail-cbdc-solutions.

MAS. 2022. BIS Innovation Hub and Central Banks of Australia, Malaysia, Singapore and South Africa Develop Experimental Multi-CBDC Platform for International Settlements. https://www.mas.gov.sg/news/media-releases/2022/experimental-multi-cbdc-platform-for-international-settlements

Mitsui & Co. 2020. Implications of China's Digital Yuan Initiative – Potential Impact and Future Focal Points. Global Strategic Studies Institute Monthly Report. https://www.mitsui.com/mgssi/en/report/detail/__icsFiles/afieldfile/2021/01/07/2011c_yatsui_e_1.pdf.

National Bank of Cambodia. 2020. Project Bakong: Next Generation Payment System. White paper. Phnom Penh. https://bakong.nbc.org.kh/download/NBC_BAKONG_White_Paper.pdf.

Newton, C. 2021. Mark in the Metaverse: Facebook's CEO on Why the Social Media Is Becoming 'A Metaverse Company'. *The Verge*. 22 July. https://www.theverge.com/22588022/mark-zuckerberg-facebook-ceo-metaverse-interview.

Nikkei Asia. 2021. Cambodia Aims to Wean Off US Dollar Dependence with Digital Currency. 4 August. https://asia.nikkei.com/Business/Markets/Currencies/Cambodia-aims-to-wean-off-US-dollar-dependence-with-digital-currency.

Office of the Controller of the Currency (US). 2021. Federally Chartered Banks and Thrifts May Participate in Independent Node Verification Networks and Use Stablecoins for Payment Activities. New release. 4 January. https://www.occ.gov/news-issuances/news-releases/2021/nr-occ-2021-2.html.

Palanivel, C. 2018. Hyperledger Iroha – Architecture Functional/Logical Flow and Consensus (YAC) Mechanism. https://www.linkedin.com/pulse/hyperledger-iroha-architecture-functionallogical-chandrasekaran/.

Park, C. Y., J. Lee, J. Villafuerte, and P. Rosenkranz. 2017. *20 Years after the Asian Financial Crisis: Lessons Learned and Future Challenges. ADB Briefs* no. 85. Manila. https://www.adb.org/sites/default/files/publication/367226/adb-brief-85.pdf.

Pei, S. 2021. Building an Integrated Digital Economy: How Asia Can Continue to Thrive in the Post-Pandemic Era. *ThinkChina*. 16 February. https://www.thinkchina.sg/building-integrated-digital-economy-how-asia-can-continue-thrive-post-pandemic-era.

People's Bank of China (PBOC). 2021. Progress of Research & Development of E-CNY in China. Working Group on E-CNY Research and Development. http://www.pbc.gov.cn/en/3688110/3688172/4157443/4293696/2021071614584691871.pdf.

PwC. 2021. PwC CBDC Global Index. https://www.pwc.com/gx/en/industries/financial-services/assets/pwc-cbdc-global-index-1st-edition-april-2021.pdf

PYMNTS. 2020. ECB President Warns Stablecoins Could 'Threaten' Monetary Sovereignty. https://www.pymnts.com/cryptocurrency/2020/ecb-president-warns-stablecoins-could-threaten-monetary-sovereignty/.

Radio Finance. 2020. Cambodia's Serey Clarifies: Bakong Is Not a Digital Currency. 11 November. https://www.radio.finance/episodes/nbcs-serey-bakong-is-not-a-cbdc-it-is-a-backbone-payment-system-built-on-dlt.

Rana, P. B. 1998. The East Asian Financial Crisis - Implications for Exchange Rate Management. ADB. http://hdl.handle.net/11540/2627.

Report to the G20. https://www.riksbank.se/globalassets/media/nyheter—pressmeddelanden/nyheter/2022/rapport-options-for-access-to-and—interoperability-of-cbdcs-for—cross-border-payments.pdf.

Richards, T., C. Thompson, and C. Dark. 2020. Retail Central Bank Digital Currency: Design Considerations, Rationales and Implications. Reserve Bank of Australia Bulletin – September 2020. https://www.rba.gov.au/publications/bulletin/2020/sep/retail-central-bank-digital-currency-design-considerations-rationales-and-implications.html.

Shiral, S. 2019. Central Bank Digital Currency: Concepts and Trends. VOX CEPR Policy Portal. https://voxeu.org/article/central-bank-digital-currency-concepts-and-trends.

Sveriges Riksbank. 2020. The Riksbank, Six Other Central Banks and BIS in Collaboration on Principles for Central Bank Digital Currency CBDC. 9 October. https://www.riksbank.se/en-gb/press-and-published/notices-and-press-releases/notices/2020/the-riksbank-six-other-central-banks-and-bis-in-collaboration-on-principles-for-central-bank-digital-currency-cbdc/.

SWIFT. 2015. The Global Adoption of Real-Time Retail Payments Systems (RT-RPS). White paper. pp. 15. https://www.swift.com/sites/default/files/documents/swift_payments_whitepaper_realtimepayments.pdf.

Wang, B. 2021. Hardware Wallets for China's Digital Yuan Sprung up During Spring Festival. *Pingwest*. 23 February. https://en.pingwest.com/a/8347.

Williamson, J. 2000. *Development of the Financial System in Post-Crisis Asia*. Manila: ADB. https://www.adb.org/sites/default/files/publication/157205/adbi-rp8.pdf.

Zhao, Wolfie. 2020. China's Digital Currency May Come with Hardware Wallets As Well. *Coinbase*. 1 February. https://www.coindesk.com/digital-yuan-hardware-wallet.

Zhou, X. 2020. Understanding China's Central Bank Digital Currency. China Finance 40 Forum. http://www.cf40.com/en/news_detail/11481.html.

Zhou, X. 2021. Digital Currency and Electronic Payment System. Economists 50 Forum. Speech in Chinese. Chinese Economists 50 Forum. http://www.50forum.org.cn/home/article/detail/id/8368.html.